# 20 EVENTS

# Events

## THAT CHANGED AMERICAN HISTORY

**LESLIE WHEELER**

**JUDITH PEACOCK**

RSVP

**RAINTREE**
**STECK-VAUGHN**
P U B L I S H E R S
The Steck-Vaughn Company

*Austin, Texas*

**Consultant:** Gary Gerstle, Department of History, The Catholic University of America

**Developed for Steck-Vaughn Company by Visual Education Corporation, Princeton, New Jersey**

Project Director:   Jewel Moulthrop
Assistant Editor:   Emilie McCardell
Researcher:   Carol Ciaston
Photo Research:   Photosearch, Inc.
Production Supervisor:   Maryellen Filipek
Proofreading Management:   Amy Davis
Word Processing:   Cynthia C. Feldner
Interior Design:   Lee Grabarczyk
Cover Design:   Maxson Crandall
Page Layout:   Maxson Crandall, Lisa R. Evans

**Raintree Steck-Vaughn Publishers staff**

Editor:   Shirley Shalit
Project Manager:   Joyce Spicer

**Library of Congress Cataloging-in-Publication Data**

Wheeler, Leslie, 1945–
    Events that changed American history / Leslie Wheeler, Judith Peacock
        p.   cm. — (20 Events)
    Includes bibliographical references and index.
    Summary: Highlights twenty events that influenced the history of the United States, including the Louisiana Purchase, the building of the transcontinental railroad, the bombing of Pearl Harbor, and the Montgomery Bus Boycott.
    ISBN 0-8114-4927-0
    1. United States—History—Miscellanea—Juvenile literature.
[1. United States—History.]   I. Peacock, Judith, 1942–.
II. Title.   III. Series.
E179.W55 1994                                                        93–19007
973—dc20                                                                   CIP
                                                                                  AC

Printed and bound in the United States

    2 3 4 5 6 7 8 9 0   VH   99 98 97 96 95 94

*Cover:* Protest against the Vietnam War increased in the United States. And as the North Vietnamese approached Saigon, Americans were evacuated by helicopter (inset) from the city.

**Credits and Acknowledgments**

**Cover photos:** The Bettmann Archive (background), UPI/Bettmann Newsphotos (inset)
**Illustrations**: American Composition and Graphics
**Maps:** Parrot Graphics

**4:** Harvey R. Phillips; **5:** Courtesy John Hancock Mutual Life Insurance Company Collection. Boston, Mass.; **7:** Library of Congress (left), Anti-Slavery Almanac (right); **8:** North Wind Pictures (left), New York Historical Society (right); **9:** U.S. Capitol Historical Society; **10:** Junius Brutus Stearns. "Washington Addressing the Constitutional Convention." Virginia Museum of Fine Arts, Richmond. Gift of Col. and Mrs. Garbisch; **11:** New York Historical Society; **12:** Independence National Historical Park Collection (left), John Trumbell. "Alexander Hamilton." Yale University Art Gallery, New Haven, Conn. (right); **13:** Ken Karp; **14:** Olaf Seltzer. "Lewis and Clark with Sacajawea and York at the Great Falls of the Missouri River," 1804. The Thomas Gilcrease Institute of American History and Art, Tulsa, Okla.; **15:** Missouri Historical Society, St. Louis; **16:** The Bettmann Archive (top), The Bettmann Archive (bottom); **17:** Gerry Gropp/© Sipa-Sport; **18:** New York Public Library (left), the Museum of the Confederacy, Richmond, Va. Photo: Katherine Wetzel (right); **19:** Library of Congress; **20:** The Bettmann Archive; **21:** Library of Congress (left), The Lincoln Museum, Fort Wayne, Indiana, a part of Lincoln National Corporation (right); **22:** National Park Service: Statue of Liberty National Monument (left), Smithsonian Institution, Washington, D.C. (right); **23:** Amtrak Photo; **24:** Courtesy of the Newberry Library, Chicago; **25:** Library of Congress; **26:** Library of Congress; **27:** Vermont State House, Montpelier (left), Courtesy of the Newberry Library, Chicago (right); **28:** National Archives; **29:** Imperial War Museum, London (left), Library of Congress (right); **30:** Library of Congress; **31:** New York Public Library; **32:** Special Collections Division, University of Washington Libraries, Seattle. Photo: James Lee #20102 (left), Library of Congress (right); **34:** Collection U.S.S. Arizona Memorial, National Park Service, Pearl Harbor, Hawaii; **35:** Library of Congress (left), UPI/Bettmann (right); **36:** Grey Villet, *Life* Magazine © Time Warner Inc.; **37:** AP/Wide World Photos; **38:** John Fitzgerald Kennedy Library, Boston, Mass.; **39:** Library of Congress (left), AP/Wide World Photos (right); **40:** National Archives; **41:** UPI/Bettmann (left); UPI/Bettmann (right); **42:** Jack Kightlinger/The White House; **43:** Vladimir Sichov, Paris

# Contents

# Plymouth Colony

★ ★ ★ ★ ★

**Pilgrim settlers planted a new colony in North America.**

## For Religious Freedom

Religious troubles racked England in the early 1600s. The English had broken away from the Roman Catholic Church and set up their own Anglican Church. By law, everyone had to belong to this church. But some English people felt that the Anglican Church was still too much like the Catholic Church. They wanted to eliminate the elaborate religious services and simplify other aspects of worship. Because these people wanted to reform, or purify, the church, they were called Puritans.

Others, called Separatists, wanted to separate from the Anglican Church altogether. Some Separatists were imprisoned and even killed for their beliefs. In 1609, a small band of Separatists left England and settled in Holland. Here they could worship freely, but they worried that their children would lose their English heritage.

The Separatists looked to America as a haven where they could practice their religion and keep their English traditions. There was already a British colony in North America—Jamestown in Virginia.

## Coming to America

In September 1620, a small ship called the *Mayflower* set sail from Plymouth, England. Of the 102 passengers on board, about half were Separatists (later known as "Pilgrims"). The rest, called "strangers," were ordinary people who hoped they would find a better life in America than they had in England. They were bound for the Virginia colony. They had with them a charter permitting them to set up their own community. The crossing was rough and the ship was overcrowded. Although many became ill, only one person died. Two children were born.

**The Mayflower Compact** Storm-tossed seas swept the *Mayflower* off its course. On November 9, the voyagers sighted land—present-day Cape Cod on the Massachusetts coast. They knew that they were far from the Virginia colony. But with so many sick and with winter fast approaching, they were eager to go ashore.

Forty-one men met in the ship's cabin to decide on a course of action. There was threatening talk of mutiny among the non-Pilgrims, those who had hoped to make their fortunes in Virginia. Instead, Pilgrims and strangers alike signed an agreement, known as the Mayflower Compact. In it they agreed to form a government and make laws that all would obey. This was the first step toward self-government in New England.

## Surviving in the Wilderness

The settlers chose the place that the Virginia colonist and explorer John Smith had labeled Plymouth on a map he had drawn. They chose their site well. There was a good water supply, and the nearby fields had been cultivated by Native Americans.

**Bound for Virginia, the *Mayflower* went off course and landed in Massachusetts. This photograph shows a reconstruction of the ship.**

Nevertheless, the first winter was filled with hardship. The settlers had little food and almost no time to build proper shelter. Half of them died from starvation, disease, and exposure to the elements.

By spring, however, conditions improved. A few friendly Indians—Squanto, Samoset, and Massasoit—showed the settlers where to hunt and fish. They also showed the settlers how to plant new crops, such as corn, squash, and beans. Without their help, the settlers would not have survived.

At the top of a hill overlooking the harbor, the settlers built a fort and meetinghouse. The meetinghouse also served as their church. Each family built a sturdy wooden house and planted a garden nearby.

By the following autumn, the settlers were ready to celebrate their success. They harvested their crops, shot wild turkey and deer, and invited the Native Americans to a three-day festival. Held in October 1621, it was the first Thanksgiving.

The Plymouth colony never became very large or very prosperous. The sandy, marshy soil at Plymouth

**With help from Native Americans and their own determination, the Pilgrims were able to survive. This painting, by Doris Lee, was made in the 1930s.**

could support only small farms. Still, the Pilgrims remained convinced that God had brought them to the New World for a purpose. As William Bradford, the second governor of the colony, later wrote in his *History of the Plimouth Plantation,* "As one small candle may light a thousand, so the light there kindled hath shone to many, yea in some sort to our whole nation."

## Colonies Grow in New England

Other settlers, mostly Puritans, followed the Pilgrims to New England. In 1630, about 1,000 people in 17 ships set sail for New England. They settled in Salem on Massachusetts Bay, but soon spread to the outlying areas and founded new towns—Boston, Cambridge, and Charlestown. These colonies grew rapidly and, by 1691, had absorbed the Plymouth colony. But the legacy of the Pilgrims survived. The New England colonies developed a strong tradition of self-government. Town meetings were a part of this tradition. Residents attended an annual meeting to discuss issues of concern and to choose *selectmen* to govern the town. As at Plymouth, the most important building in many New England towns was the meetinghouse. Religious traditions also remained strong in the New England colonies.

As the colonies expanded, however, relations between the settlers and the Indians worsened. The Puritans who came to New England viewed the natives as savages who needed to be civilized through Christianity and European traditions. The English attitude toward the Indians was generally disapproving and often cruel. This attitude led to much open conflict in the years that followed.

*...Having agreed ... to plant the first colony in the northern parts of Virginia, [we] do seriously and together in the presence of God, and one another, combine ourselves together into a political body. We do this ... to enact and plan such just and equal laws, rules, acts, and offices, from time to time, as shall be thought best for the general good of the colony. Unto which we promise all due submission and obedience.*

*11th of November*
*Anno Domini 1620*

**In this excerpt from the Mayflower Compact, the colonists set forth the idea of self-government, a tradition still continued in New England's town meetings.**

# The Introduction of Slavery

★ ★ ★ ★ ★

**Colonists began importing Africans as slaves to meet a severe labor shortage.**

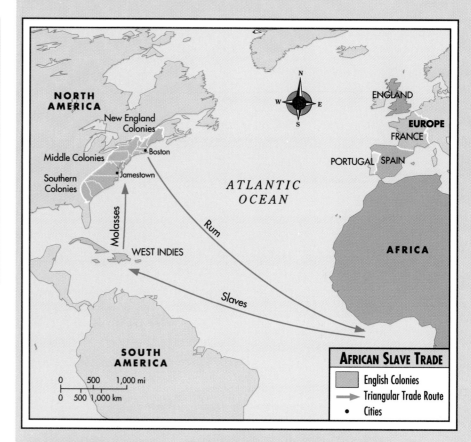

**AFRICAN SLAVE TRADE**
- English Colonies
- → Triangular Trade Route
- • Cities

A triangular pattern of trade developed. Rum and other goods were transported to Africa, where they were exchanged for African people. About six percent of the slaves brought from Africa went to the Southern colonies to work on the plantations.

## Help Wanted: Laborers

In the 17th century, the New World was rich in resources but short on laborers. Settlers in the Spanish colonies attempted—with little success—to force Indians to work in the gold and silver mines and on the sugar and tobacco plantations.

The English settlers used white indentured servants. Each servant, before leaving England, signed a contract promising to work for a master for a certain length of time. In return, the servant received free passage across the Atlantic. As soon as most indentured servants had fulfilled their contracts, they became free to work for themselves. However, indentured servants proved to be an unruly work force. Many began to demand their freedom before their contracts expired.

Slaves from Africa were another source of labor. The slave trade had started in the 16th century. Portuguese ships began transporting slaves captured on the west coast of Africa to Portuguese colonies in the New World. Few Europeans objected to the enslavement of Africans, because most believed that they were uncivilized heathens, or non-Christians.

## Slavery Takes Hold in America

In 1619, the first Africans arrived in Jamestown, Virginia, aboard a Dutch ship. They were sold to the colonists as laborers. They were treated as indentured servants and freed after their term of service.

By about 1640, however, there were a few thousand slaves in Virginia. And by the mid-1700s, slavery had spread to all of the 13 colonies—approximately 250,000 slaves in all. Slavery, however, was more widespread in the South, where slave labor was used on the large tobacco and rice plantations. Agriculture in the Northern colonies consisted of small farms, which did not require large numbers of slaves. Yet Northern merchants made huge profits from the slave trade.

**The Slave Trade** Ambitious New England sea captains developed a "triangular trade" involving rum, slaves, and sugar. They took rum and other goods—cloth, beads, guns—to West Africa, where they traded for slaves.

The voyage back to the Americas became infamous as the "middle passage." Chained together, hundreds of Africans were jammed into the filthy, foul-smelling holds of ships. They were unable to stand upright. There wasn't enough air to breathe. And they received only a small amount of food and drink. Many died of disease along the way. Their bodies were thrown overboard. Some, during the brief period they were allowed on deck, committed suicide by hurling themselves into the sea and drowning.

Those who survived the trip were traded for molasses in the West

**Most Africans ended up as field slaves, working hard for long hours under the eye of an overseer.**

## Slavery and Antislavery

The slave population grew rapidly in the South. By the mid-1700s, slaves made up nearly half of Virginia's population. In South Carolina, slaves outnumbered whites two to one.

As slavery became strongly established, opposition to the system increased. Thomas Jefferson, himself a slave owner, attacked the slave trade. He said that it was contrary to the principles of the American Revolution. But no protest against slavery was included in the Declaration of Independence. When the Constitution was written, slavery was allowed to continue. In the first half of the 19th century, Northern opposition to slavery grew. Controversy flared over whether slavery would be introduced to newly acquired territory west of the Mississippi. Congress attempted to deal with the issue through a series of compromises. But the debate only intensified. Eventually slavery and states' rights became the main issues over which the Civil War was fought. The institution was finally abolished in that war, and all slaves were freed. Nevertheless, slavery left scars of prejudice and inequality that have lasted to the present day.

**Some slaves were granted their freedom before 1865, but this freedom was not universally recognized. This picture shows the kidnapping of a freedman.**

Indies. Molasses, which is made from sugarcane, was taken back to the colonies and made into rum.

**The Slave System** As large numbers of slaves were brought into the colonies, colonial legislatures passed laws that became known as slave codes. These laws regulated almost every aspect of the slave's life, giving the master complete control. Slaves could not leave their owner's property without a pass. They could not gather in groups without a white person present. Laws in some colonies made it a crime to teach a slave to read or write.

The introduction of African slaves expanded the plantation system in the South. Wealthy planters bought the best land and used gangs of slaves to work it. Using slave labor enabled planters to build fine houses, modeled on English estates. They sent their sons to England to be educated. And they lived like nobility.

Because slaves were valuable property, they were usually given adequate food, clothing, and housing. But slave owners were also eager to get as much work from their slaves as possible. Most slaves were field hands, who worked long hours and often at the mercy of brutal overseers. Some slaves resisted by work slowdowns and acts of sabotage. Others ran away. A few tried to escape their condition by outright rebellion. But rebellions had little chance of success. The white population was well armed and numerous enough to defeat all assaults on the slave system.

# The Declaration of Independence

★ ★ ★ ★ ★

**Colonists proclaimed the independence of a new nation in which the people, rather than a king, would rule.**

## Unfair Taxation!

In the 1760s, the British imposed a series of taxes on the colonists in America to help pay the costs of maintaining their empire. The colonists deeply resented these taxes. They felt that since the British Parliament did not truly represent them, it had no right to tax them.

The colonists protested the Stamp Act of 1765, which put a tax on legal documents and newspapers, by refusing to buy British goods. Parliament repealed the Stamp Act but passed a new tax on tea and other items.

On March 5, 1770, a Boston mob shouted insults and threw rock-filled snowballs at a group of British soldiers. The soldiers panicked and fired into the mob, killing five Bostonians in what became known as the Boston Massacre.

Parliament then revoked all the taxes except the one on tea. On March 16, 1773, a group of patriots, disguised as Indians, boarded three British ships and dumped 342 chests of tea into the harbor. Parliament punished Boston for the so-called Boston Tea Party with harsh new laws, which the colonists dubbed the Intolerable Acts. Outraged colonists called for a congress, or meeting. And in September 1774, delegates from 12 colonies met in Philadelphia. This First Continental Congress sent a petition to King George III demanding the repeal of the Intolerable Acts. It also called for a new boycott of British goods. Some of the more radical delegates wanted the colonies to become independent of Great Britain.

Meanwhile, in Massachusetts, local militia—called Minutemen—began gathering gunpowder and drilling on village greens. On April 18, 1775, British troops set out to seize a supply of weapons at Concord and to capture rebel leaders. Alerted by Paul Revere and William Dawes, the militia met the British at Lexington. Here the first shots were fired. A second, brief battle at Concord forced the British to retreat.

The Second Continental Congress began meeting in Philadelphia. Most delegates hoped to resolve their differences with Britain, but a few urged independence. In June, the bloody Battle of Bunker Hill, again near Boston, fueled the growing desire for independence. So did the publication in January 1776 of the pamphlet *Common Sense*. Its author, Thomas Paine, argued persuasively in favor of separation from Britain. He also presented convincing arguments supporting the replacement of the monarchy (rule of a king or queen) with democracy (rule of the people).

**Before signing the declaration, Congress called for certain changes, such as the removal of a passage condemning the slave trade.**

**Although there were some dissenters, most people cheered the declaration and the end of King George III's rule.**

## Independence Is Declared

By June 1776, the Second Continental Congress was ready to make the final break with Britain. The delegates appointed a committee to draft a declaration of independence. The committee included John Adams, Benjamin Franklin, and Thomas Jefferson.

**Jefferson Drafts a Statement** At 33, Jefferson was the youngest member of the committee. Yet the task of preparing the draft fell to this tall, handsome Virginian. The Declaration of Independence had two main parts. The first section explained why people have a right to rebel. It also described the ideas behind the new republican form of government that the Americans intended to establish. These ideas about equality and basic human rights came from French, British, and Scottish philosophers—Montesquieu, Locke, and Hutcheson. But Jefferson expressed them in a way that made them immortal: "We hold these truths to be self-evident, that all men are created equal."

Jefferson then stated that government is a compact between the people and their rulers. According to this theory, all people have certain basic rights—"life, liberty, and the pursuit of happiness." Governments are formed to protect these rights, "deriving their just powers from the consent of the governed." But when a government violates this compact, the people have the right to dissolve that government and to form a new one.

The second part of the declaration consisted of a long list of grievances against the English king. The final paragraph referred to the colonies as "the United States of America" for the first time.

**With French help, the Americans forced the British to surrender at Yorktown, the last major battle in the war for independence. A new nation was born.**

## The War for Independence

The Declaration of Independence committed the colonies to a full-scale war with Britain. It brought aid from abroad and provided an opportunity for France to intervene on the side of the Americans against the British. At the same time, the declaration divided Americans into *patriots*, who were committed to independence, and *loyalists,* who remained loyal to Great Britain. As many as a third of Americans remained in the loyalist camp.

In the year following the declaration, the colonists' Continental Army suffered a series of crushing defeats. Then, in the summer of 1777, it won an important victory at Saratoga, New York. The British had failed in their attempt to cut off New England from the rest of the colonies.

The British concentrated their next efforts in the South, where, with loyalist help, they won several battles. By late 1780, the tide began to turn in favor of the Americans. On October 19, 1781, the British army of 6,000 surrendered at Yorktown, Virginia. As little fighting followed, the war for independence was essentially over. It took two more years for the British to formally grant independence, in the Treaty of Paris. But a new nation had been born.

# Ratification of the Constitution

★ ★ ★ ★ ★

**The blueprint for American government is the oldest constitution in the world.**

## The Confederation Is Weak

In the last years of the war for independence, the Americans created a new government. The Articles of Confederation, approved in 1781, set up a loose organization of states under a central government with very limited powers. The weaknesses of the new government were soon glaringly apparent.

In 1783, angry Revolutionary War veterans marched on Philadelphia to demand the back pay owed them. The frightened members of Congress fled to Princeton, New Jersey. The Congress—the national government—lacked funds because it had no power to tax the people directly. It had to depend on the states for money.

In 1786, trouble erupted in Massachusetts when enraged farmers, led by Daniel Shays, attempted to seize the arsenal in Springfield. Their land was being taken away for failure to pay their debts. They wanted the government to issue paper money, which would enable them to pay their creditors. Shays' Rebellion was put down. But it convinced many Americans of the need for a stronger government.

## The Creation of a New Government

In May 1787, delegates from all the states except Rhode Island gathered anxiously in Philadelphia. They had come to revise the Articles of Confederation. But by the end of four months, they had drafted an entirely new plan for government. They chose George Washington, the Revolutionary War hero, to preside over the convention. And to encourage freedom of discussion, they pledged themselves to secrecy. Even so, there were times during the long, hot months of debate when the convention came close to dissolving. But it did not break up, mainly because of the delegates' ability to compromise.

One major compromise concerned representation. The small states wanted each state to have one vote in Congress. The large states, however, believed that representation should be based on population. The delegates compromised by creating two legislative bodies. Representation in the lower house of Congress would be based on population. In the upper house, or Senate, each state would be equally represented by two senators.

The second important compromise involved slavery. Southerners wanted slaves included in the population counts. Northerners argued that slaves should then be taxed at the same rate as citizens. Finally, the delegates decided that for the purposes of taxation and representation, each slave would be counted as three-fifths of a person. Southerners also won a delay in the clause abolishing slavery. Although slavery continued into the 1860s, the importation of slaves was made illegal in 1808.

**Checks and Balances** The Constitution set up a federal system in which the central government shares power with the state governments. The central government was divided into three branches—legislative, executive, and judicial. Each branch was expected to check (restrain) and balance the power of the others.

**When Washington presented the Constitution to the delegates, he spoke on its behalf. He said that the choice was between the Constitution and disunion.**

**The Fight for Ratification** The publication of the proposed Constitution sparked instant debate. Those who supported the Constitution and a strong central government were known as Federalists. Their opponents were labeled Anti-Federalists. The Anti-Federalists feared that the Constitution would result in tyranny.

These two groups often waged bitter battles in each state to ratify, or approve, the Constitution. The Federalists won support for their cause through a series of brilliant newspaper articles called the *Federalist Papers*. Alexander Hamilton, James Madison, and John Jay wrote the articles. Although the Federalists were better organized, the contest was a close one.

For the Constitution to become law, 9 of the 13 states had to approve it. Delaware ratified the document first, in December 1787. New Hampshire was the ninth state to ratify, in June 1788. But the future of the new government was uncertain without Virginia and New York, two of the largest and wealthiest states. They still had not decided. In Virginia, a fiery patriot turned Anti-Federalist, Patrick Henry, squared off against the calm and thoughtful James Madison. Madison's arguments carried the day. Persuaded by the Federalist victory in Virginia, New York and the remaining states finally voted in favor of ratification.

## After Ratification

In 1788, citizens in each state elected representatives and senators. And to no one's surprise, George Washington was selected as President—by unanimous vote.

The Anti-Federalists who still had doubts about the Constitution were reassured by the addition of ten amendments, known as the Bill of Rights, in 1791. The first nine amendments protected such individual liberties as the right to a trial by jury and freedom of religion, speech, and the press. The 10th Amendment reserved to the states all powers not specifically granted to the federal government.

The framers of the Constitution had acted wisely. The system of government they created has lasted for more than 200 years, with the addition of only 16 more amendments.

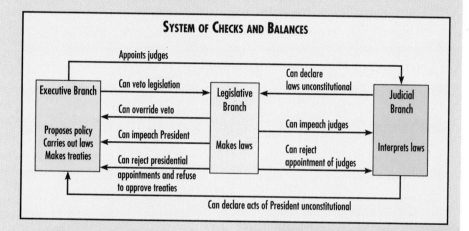

**SYSTEM OF CHECKS AND BALANCES**

Appoints judges

Executive Branch — Can veto legislation → Legislative Branch — Can declare laws unconstitutional → Judicial Branch

Can override veto

Proposes policy
Carries out laws
Makes treaties

Can impeach President

Makes laws

Can impeach judges

Interprets laws

Can reject presidential appointments and refuse to approve treaties

Can reject appointment of judges

Can declare acts of President unconstitutional

▲ By giving each branch of government some power over the other branches, the delegates created a system that would prevent one branch of government from becoming more powerful than the others.

▼ Washington, shown here at his inauguration, was the unanimous choice of the delegates. It was later said that he was "first in war, first in peace, and first in the hearts of his countrymen."

# The 1800 Election

★ ★ ★ ★ ★

**The transfer of power to a new President confirmed the stability of the new republic.**

## Before the 1800 Election

The Constitution does not mention political parties. Furthermore, President George Washington worked hard to prevent their rise. Yet by 1791, two opposing governing factions, or groups, had sprung up. These factions hardened into political parties because of their differing opinions about economic policy, foreign affairs, and the way the nation should be governed. The Federalists, led by Alexander Hamilton, favored a strong central government; and they sought to strengthen business and industry. They also favored close ties with England rather than with France.

Under the leadership of Thomas Jefferson and James Madison, the Democratic-Republicans believed in a central government with limited powers. They envisioned a nation of small farmers. They also greatly admired the ideals of human equality of the French Revolution. These ideals seemed to promise the ordinary French citizens more control of their government than Americans of the time possessed.

The two parties attacked each other violently in the newspapers. Washington's decision to serve a second term prevented a confrontation in 1792. Four years later, John Adams (a Federalist) was elected President and Thomas Jefferson (a Democratic-Republican) was elected Vice-President. Leaders of both parties looked ahead to the election of 1800 with uneasiness.

## The "Revolution of 1800"

John Adams was not a popular President. During his term, the nation almost went to war with France. Moreover, by passing the Alien and Sedition Acts, the Federalists threatened individual liberties. They used the Sedition Act, which made it a crime to print anything "false, scandalous, or malicious" about the government, to attempt to gag the Democratic-Republican press.

**The Candidates** Besides attacking their opponents, the Federalists quarreled among themselves. By 1800, they were seriously divided. John Adams barely won his party's nomination for reelection.

The Democratic-Republicans, on the other hand, rallied behind Thomas Jefferson. Though a wealthy Virginian, Jefferson championed the cause of the common people. His running mate was Aaron Burr, a brilliant but unscrupulous New York politician.

Like the previous campaign, this one was waged not by the candidates personally but through newspaper

**Thomas Jefferson (*left*) and Alexander Hamilton (*right*) were the leading exponents of two opposite views of government, which eventually became two political parties.**

### MAJOR U.S. POLITICAL PARTIES

| Year | Jefferson's Principles | Hamilton's Principles |
|------|------------------------|------------------------|
| *1791 | Democratic-Republicans | Federalists |
| *1816 | | End of Federalists |
| *1820 | Republicans (One party for about five years) | |
| *1825 | Democratic-Republicans | National Republicans |
| 1834 | Democrats | Whigs |
| 1854 | | Republicans |
| Present | | |

\* These parties were engaged in political activities around these dates.

Note: Various third parties appeared in some elections, but parties shown here dominated political life.

attacks that were often vicious. The Federalists charged that if Jefferson were elected, he would introduce the radical ideas of the French Revolution. The other side accused the Federalists of trying to establish a tyranny. In the end, the Democratic-Republicans were victorious—but in a way no one had anticipated.

Under the system set up by the Constitution, the President was chosen by an *electoral college* consisting of *electors* from every state. The candidate with the most electoral votes became President; the candidate with the second highest number of votes became Vice-President. In 1796, this system had given the nation a President and Vice-President from different parties. In 1800, it resulted in a tie between the two Democratic-Republican candidates, Burr and Jefferson. Each had received 73 votes; Adams had received 65 votes.

**Deadlock in the House** Since Burr made no move to step aside, the election went to the House of Representatives. In the House, which the Federalists controlled, each state had one vote. Most Federalists voted for Burr, and the first ballot ended in another tie!

It took five tense days and 35 ballots before the tie was finally broken. Alexander Hamilton broke the deadlock. Much as he disliked Jefferson, he hated Burr more. With Hamilton's support, Jefferson finally won the election.

**Jefferson's Inauguration** Thomas Jefferson took the oath of office on March 4, 1801. John Adams and many other Federalists stayed away from the ceremony. In his inaugural address, Jefferson called for unity and an end to the fighting between the two parties. "We are all Federalists, we are all Republicans," he said. In fact, as President, Jefferson not only preserved the major accomplishments of the Federalists, he strengthened them as well.

## After the 1800 Election

The election had revealed a problem with the electoral system. Two years later, Congress proposed a constitutional amendment to remedy this problem. The 12th Amendment provided separate balloting for the President and the Vice-President in the electoral college.

More importantly, the election of 1800 marked the official beginning of the two-party system. For the first time since the establishment of the new government, a change in leadership had occurred. One party had transferred power to another. And this transfer had taken place in a peaceful, orderly fashion. There was none of the bloodshed that often accompanied the rise of a new ruler.

Instead, the election of 1800 demonstrated that the new republic was to be a government based on law, rather than on the changing fortunes of particular individuals or groups. This was the most revolutionary feature of "the revolution of 1800."

The struggle between the Federalists and Democratic-Republicans gave rise to the two-party system. With the growth of political parties came a new industry—election souvenirs.

# The Louisiana Purchase

★ ★ ★ ★ ★

This land purchase doubled the size of the United States and spurred territorial expansion.

## The Great Wilderness

In 1800, the mighty Mississippi River formed the western boundary of the United States. From the river to the Rocky Mountains, and from the Gulf of Mexico to Canada, stretched a vast territory called Louisiana. This land had once belonged to France but now belonged to Spain. The French ruler, Napoleon Bonaparte, had dreams of an empire in North America, and he wanted Louisiana back. Napoleon persuaded Spain to sign a secret treaty returning Louisiana to France.

Learning of this secret treaty, President Jefferson became alarmed. He hoped that Louisiana would some-day be part of an "American Empire for Liberty." He was already planning an expedition to explore the territory. French control of the port of New Orleans troubled Jefferson even more. American settlers living west of the Appalachian Mountains depended on having access to New Orleans. They needed that port to get their produce to overseas markets.

## Buying Louisiana

Jefferson instructed Robert Livingston, the American minister to France, to buy the land at the mouth of the Mississippi. If necessary, he was to buy New Orleans and the lands on the east bank of the river, which were then called West Florida. Congress had authorized Livingston to spend $2 million. Jefferson sent James Monroe to assist Livingston with these sensitive negotiations. Expecting resistance to their offer, the two Americans were astonished when Napoleon offered to sell all of Louisiana for $15 million!

Napoleon had changed his plans for several reasons:

- His failure to put down a revolt in the French West Indies destroyed his dream of an empire in North America.

- He was planning a war against England and needed money.

- He could not risk a showdown with the United States.

Napoleon's amazing offer left Livingston and Monroe momentarily confused. They had no authority to spend so much money. Nor did they have a clear idea how much land they were buying. But if they hesitated, Napoleon might change his mind and retract his offer. So in April 1803, Livingston and Monroe signed the treaty by which the United States acquired Louisiana.

**A Constitutional Amendment or Not?** The Louisiana Purchase came with headaches, along with high hopes, for Jefferson. He believed in a strict interpretation of the Constitution. And nothing in that document gave the President the right to acquire that much new territory. Jefferson felt that an amendment might be necessary. But if he delayed, the deal might collapse. Its failure would disappoint him and the western settlers, who were urging approval for the treaty.

**Lewis and Clark at Black Eagle Falls, in what is now Montana, with their Shoshone guide, Sacajawea, and Clark's servant, York.**

Finally Jefferson decided that the President's war and treaty-making powers included the right to acquire territory. On October 20, 1803, an enthusiastic Senate approved the purchase. The United States acquired about 828,000 square miles, doubling its size at a cost of approximately 18 dollars per square mile!

## The Lewis and Clark Expedition

In the spring of 1804, Jefferson put into action his plan for an expedition into the Louisiana Territory. Meriwether Lewis and William Clark led a band of 50 on a thrilling adventure. Pushing off from St. Louis, they headed northwest on the Missouri River. By winter, they had reached the land of the Mandan Indians in present-day North Dakota. They built a fort and waited for the snows to melt. In the spring, the Lewis and Clark expedition set out again. They had with them a young Shoshone woman, Sacajawea, who served as their guide and interpreter. With her infant son strapped to her back, Sacajawea guided the expedition through the towering, jagged barrier of the Rocky Mountains and along the rapidly flowing waters of the Snake, Salmon, and Columbia rivers. Finally, in November 1805, the explorers looked with awe upon "this great Pacific Ocean, which we have been so long anxious to see." After nearly two years, the Lewis and Clark expedition returned with detailed maps, journals, and drawings of the region's geography, plant and animal life, and inhabitants.

▲ The expedition took two years and provided detailed information, drawings, and maps of the previously unknown territory. This is a page from Clark's diary.

▼ The purchase of the Louisiana Territory doubled the size of the United States. Thirteen states were carved out of the territory.

## Thirteen New States

The Louisiana Purchase ensured America's future growth. The nation gained control of the Mississippi River and a network of waterways that were vital to trade and settlement. It also acquired a vast, fertile land of plains and forests. Jefferson's dream of a nation of independent farmers now seemed attainable.

Indeed, the ink on the treaty was barely dry when settlers began pouring into the new territory. A territorial government was set up. In 1812, the new state of Louisiana gained admission to the Union. It was the first of 13 states that would be carved from the Louisiana Territory.

The Louisiana Purchase also spurred the push to the Pacific. Rugged fur trappers penetrated the Rockies and pressed into Oregon and California. Eager settlers followed. By the 1840s, many Americans had come to believe that it was their "Manifest Destiny," or clear right, to expand the "empire of liberty" to the entire continent.

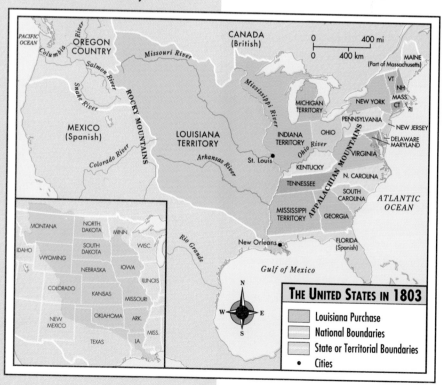

# The Seneca Falls Convention

★ ★ ★ ★ ★

This meeting, in 1848, launched the movement that would help women win full citizenship.

## Second-Class Citizenship

A spirit of reform swept the United States in the period from 1830 to 1860. Americans were convinced that the world could and should be made better. They organized and crusaded to abolish, or end, slavery, improve public education and the care of the mentally ill, and eliminate the evils of alcohol.

American women participated in many of these crusades, especially the temperance movement (the effort to end alcohol use) and abolition. Their involvement in reform made them keenly aware of their own inferior status.

In the 19th century, women were second-class citizens. Married women could not own property in their own names or even make a will without their husbands' approval. Opportunities for education and employment were limited. Single women might teach or work in factories. But they were paid lower wages than men. Married women were expected to devote themselves to home and family. For women to even speak in public, let alone vote, was unthinkable—until a group of strong-minded women challenged the way things were.

## The Women's Rights Movement Begins

In 1840, two angry women made a vow. One was Lucretia Mott, a Quaker preacher and abolitionist. The other was Elizabeth Cady Stanton, the young bride of a prominent abolitionist. Mott and Stanton met for the first time at the World's Antislavery Convention in London. Although Mott had come as a delegate to the convention, she was not allowed to participate in the proceedings because of her sex. Mott and Stanton vowed then that when they returned to the United States, they would organize a convention to address the long-ignored issue of women's rights.

**Meeting at Seneca Falls** Eight years later, Mott and Stanton's convention took place. On July 19, 1848, 240 people, including 40 men, crowded into the hot, stuffy Methodist chapel in Seneca Falls, New York. They listened enthusiastically to the reading of a Declaration of Sentiments and Resolutions. The declaration, modeled after the Declaration of Independence, boldly stated "that all men and women are created equal." The declaration went on to list the "injuries and usurpations," or taking without right, that women had suffered at the hands of men, and ended with a series of resolutions calling for equal rights.

The women and men at Seneca Falls debated each resolution and passed each unanimously—except for

**As Susan B. Anthony worked to protect the rights of others, she realized that women's rights had been ignored.**

**It took more than 80 years of demonstrations like this one for women's voting rights to become the law of the land.**

one, the right to vote. Many at the convention, including Mott herself, considered the demand too radical. But Stanton, who had proposed the resolution, stood her ground. And with the support of Frederick Douglass, a former slave turned abolitionist, the convention finally approved this first official call for women's suffrage (the right to vote).

**Susan B. Anthony** The Seneca Falls Convention marked the beginning of nearly a century of struggle. National women's rights conventions were held every year until the outbreak of the Civil War. And hundreds of women joined the cause.

Among them was Susan B. Anthony, a young Quaker temperance worker from Rochester, New York. Stanton was the movement's radical thinker, and Lucy Stone was its most eloquent spokesperson. But Anthony was the movement's organizational genius. Her tireless work organizing conventions, petition campaigns, and various lobbying efforts earned her the reputation of the "Napoleon" of women's rights.

Some people called 1992 the "Year of the Woman." It was the year in which an unprecedented number of women were elected to Congress. California's new senators, Barbara Boxer (*left*) and Diane Feinstein (*right*) are shown here.

## Progress Is Slow but Steady

By 1900, women had made some important gains. Several states had passed laws giving married women the right to own property. Some states had also passed less restrictive divorce laws.

Women had greater access to higher education. After the Civil War, women's colleges such as Vassar, Wellesley, and Smith opened. State universities in the Midwest began to admit women. Many in this new generation of college-educated women sought careers outside the home. More women entered the legal and medical professions. This trend has continued.

By 1900, women in Utah, Wyoming, Colorado, and Idaho had the right to vote. But they could vote only

in state and local elections; the Constitution still barred them from casting ballots in national elections. In 1890, two women's suffrage organizations joined forces to form the National American Woman Suffrage Association. This new organization worked hard to gain voting rights through amendments to state constitutions and an amendment to the United States Constitution. As the determined Susan B. Anthony declared not long before her death in 1906, "Failure is impossible."

In 1920, the 19th Amendment to the Constitution, giving women the right to vote in all elections, was finally ratified, or approved. Nearly 75 years had passed since the first public demand for women's suffrage had been made at Seneca Falls. Stanton, Mott, Anthony, and other leaders had died. Yet one woman who had journeyed to Seneca Falls that historic day in 1848, Charlotte Woodward—then 19 years old—lived to vote in the 1920 presidential election.

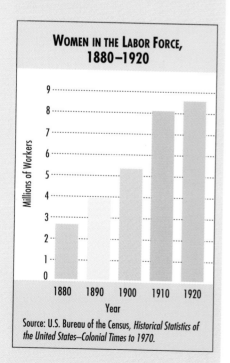

### WOMEN IN THE LABOR FORCE, 1880–1920

Millions of Workers

(bar graph with values for years 1880, 1890, 1900, 1910, 1920 on a scale from 0 to 9)

Source: U.S. Bureau of the Census, *Historical Statistics of the United States—Colonial Times to 1970.*

As women were given greater access to education and jobs, they sought careers outside the home.

# Secession
★ ★ ★ ★ ★

**By creating a separate nation, the South began a long and terrible war.**

## Conflict and Compromise

In the first half of the 19th century, the North and South grew increasingly divided over many issues. But disagreement over slavery was the central area of conflict. The North was rapidly becoming a region of cities and factories based on the labor of free workers. But the South was largely rural and agricultural, with slaves making up most of its labor force. Many Northerners believed that slavery was morally wrong. Many Southerners feared that without slave labor, their economic base would collapse.

In 1819, the differences between the two sections reached a crisis point when Missouri asked to be admitted to the Union as a slave state. At the time there were 15 slave states and 15 free states. Missouri's admission would upset this balance. Northerners proposed banning slavery in Missouri. Southerners protested vigorously. Finally, in 1820, both sides hammered out a compromise. Missouri would be admitted as a slave state, and Maine as a free state. The so-called Missouri Compromise also barred slavery from the rest of the Louisiana Territory.

In the 1850s, a series of crises shattered the uneasy peace of the Missouri Compromise. California's request to join the Union as a free state threatened the balance once again. And again Congress compromised. California could come in free, but slavery was permitted in the rest of the territory won from Mexico in 1848, if the people living there wanted it. Congress also passed a tougher law about runaway slaves, which required their return to their masters.

Then, in 1854, Congress passed the Kansas-Nebraska Act. This law violated the principle of the Missouri Compromise by allowing the people of these territories to make up their own minds about slavery. The new law led to bloodshed, as Northerners and Southerners struggled for control of Kansas. It also contributed to the emergence of the Republican Party, a new political party that took a stand against slavery in the territories.

In 1857, the Supreme Court issued a decision in the Dred Scott case. The decision, a bitter disappointment to Northern abolitionists, held that Congress could not prohibit slavery in the territories. Two years later, Southerners were horrified when John Brown, a Northern abolitionist, led a raid at Harpers Ferry, Virginia, in the hope of inciting a slave rebellion.

▲ A Charleston newspaper summed up the situation with this headline when the South seceded.

▶ After the Union garrison at Fort Sumter surrendered, the South seized the fort and raised the Confederate flag. War had begun.

**Lincoln's Election** As the election of 1860 approached, feeling ran high on both sides. The Republicans chose Abraham Lincoln, a moderate, as their candidate. Their platform called for barring slavery from the territories, instituting high tariffs (which would benefit the North), giving free land to western settlers, and building a transcontinental railroad. Slavery split the Democrats into two factions, each with its own candidate. Northern Democrats rallied behind Stephen A. Douglas. He supported letting the people of a territory decide about slavery. Southern Democrats nominated John Breckinridge of Kentucky. He wanted federal protection for slavery in the territories. A fourth party, the Constitutional Union Party, chose John Bell of Tennessee as its candidate and sought to preserve the Union.

Voting went by region. Breckinridge won the South, Lincoln the North and West. Lincoln's success gave him enough electoral votes to win the presidency.

This photograph of Civil War casualties, taken at the 1862 Battle of Antietam, made vivid the grim realities of war.

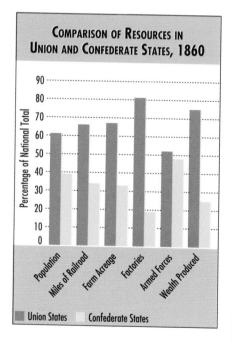

COMPARISON OF RESOURCES IN UNION AND CONFEDERATE STATES, 1860

Percentage of National Total

Population, Miles of Railroad, Farm Acreage, Factories, Armed Forces, Wealth Produced

■ Union States  ■ Confederate States

The North surpassed the South in several important ways, including population and industrial production.

## Secession

Having threatened to act if Lincoln were elected, South Carolina voted to secede, or leave the Union, on December 20, 1860. Six other Southern states quickly followed. In February 1861, the states that had seceded formed the Confederate States of America. They adopted a constitution guaranteeing slavery and emphasizing the right of individual states to control their own destiny.

Many Southerners did not believe that the North would fight to keep them in the Union. If war occurred, they were convinced the South would win. Lincoln warned that the federal government would defend any forts not yet seized by the Confederates. Despite this warning, Southern troops opened fire on Fort Sumter, in Charleston harbor, on April 12, 1861, and forced its surrender.

To President Lincoln, this was an act of outright rebellion. He promptly called on the states loyal to the Union to provide him with troops to quell the insurrection. Meanwhile four more Southern states joined the Confederacy. The stage was set for a long, bloody war.

## War and Devastation

The conflict between the Union and the Confederacy lasted four terrible years. It finally ended when Confederate general Robert E. Lee surrendered at Appomattox Court House, Virginia, on April 9, 1865. About 360,000 Union soldiers and 260,000 Confederate soldiers died. Civilian casualties were also numerous. One was Lincoln, killed by an assassin's bullet, less than a week after Lee's surrender.

In the South, the devastation was enormous. Cities lay in ruins and farms, homes, and businesses were completely destroyed. The biggest change, however, was that slavery had been abolished.

The United States became a single nation again, one now based on the labor of free people. The Civil War marked the victory of a strong federal government over the power of individual states. It sparked the growth of cities and the further rise of industry in the North. And it left a legacy of anger and bitterness in the South. By freeing the African American slaves, the war righted a great wrong. But it would be decades before Blacks were able to enjoy the full rights of citizenship.

# The Emancipation Proclamation

★ ★ ★ ★ ★

**A presidential decree turned the Civil War into a crusade against slavery.**

135,000 SETS, 270,000 VOLUMES SOLD.

# UNCLE TOM'S CABIN

## FOR SALE HERE.

AN EDITION FOR THE MILLION, COMPLETE IN 1 Vol., PRICE 37 1-2 CENTS.
"        "        IN GERMAN, IN 1 Vol., PRICE 50 CENTS.
"        "        IN 2 Vols., CLOTH, 6 PLATES, PRICE $1.50.
SUPERB ILLUSTRATED EDITION, IN 1 Vol., WITH 153 ENGRAVINGS.
PRICES FROM $2.50 TO $5.00.

## The Greatest Book of the Age.

*Harriet Beecher Stowe's novel added fuel to the slavery debate and aggravated tensions between North and South.*

## Mounting Pressure

At the outset, President Abraham Lincoln made it very clear that the North was fighting the Civil War to preserve the Union. Freeing the slaves was not part of the goal. Although the President personally opposed slavery, he took a moderate position to keep the slaveholding border states in the Union. Also, he didn't think that the federal government could abolish slavery, since it was legal under the Constitution. Finally, the President was concerned about how four million freed slaves would fit into the nation's social and economic life.

But as the war progressed, Lincoln faced mounting pressure from abolitionists and radical Republicans in Congress to emancipate, or free, the slaves. In May 1861, a Union general refused to return slaves who had escaped to join the Union side. In April 1862, Congress abolished slavery in the District of Columbia. Then it passed laws that freed all slaves in the territories, slaves who had escaped from their Confederate masters, and runaway slaves who had been captured by Union troops.

## Lincoln Issues His Famous Decree

**A War Measure** By the summer of 1862, Lincoln had become convinced that emancipation was necessary for military reasons. The war was not going well for the Union. Its armies had suffered a string of defeats on the battlefield. It also faced the alarming prospect that Britain and France might intervene on the side of the Confederacy. To keep this from happening and to strike a crippling blow at the South, Lincoln decided that the slaves must be freed.

But Lincoln did not want emancipation to look like an act of desperation—as it might, given the North's battle losses. So he waited until after the Union victory at Antietam in September 1862 before issuing a warning.

He warned that if the Confederacy did not surrender by January 1, 1863, he would declare its slaves "then, thenceforth, and forever free."

When January 1 came with no reply from the Confederacy, Lincoln issued the proclamation. It freed the slaves in the states that were in rebellion against the Union. But it excluded slaves in the border states and in those parts of the Confederacy that were already under Union control. In effect, the Emancipation Proclamation did not free any slaves immediately.

**"A New Birth of Freedom"** Nevertheless, the decree had an enormous impact. As word of the proclamation spread, growing numbers of slaves fled to the Union lines. Since the proclamation gave Union generals the

African Americans cheered Lincoln's arrival in Richmond. More than 180,000 newly freed Blacks served in the Union Army.

The pain of the long and terrible war shows on Lincoln's face in this portrait, taken four days before he was assassinated.

authority to recruit former slaves as soldiers, thousands swelled the ranks of the Union armies. The South, on the other hand, lost much of its labor force—the slaves who were needed to work on the plantations. Without them, the Southern economy would be damaged.

Even more importantly, the Emancipation Proclamation turned the tide of the war by changing it into a great moral crusade against slavery. The proclamation aroused anti-slavery sentiment in England and France, making it more difficult for these countries to consider supporting the Confederacy. And the Union was inspired by a new and higher purpose. As Lincoln stated in his Gettysburg Address, the war was being fought for "a new birth of freedom."

## Legalizing Freedom

Fearing that the proclamation might not be legal once the war was ended, Lincoln and others pushed for a constitutional amendment abolishing slavery everywhere in the nation. The 13th Amendment, ratified in December 1865, accomplished this. Congress also established a Freedmen's Bureau to help the former slaves find jobs and get an education, and to protect them from racial discrimination. Congress also passed two other amendments to protect the rights of Blacks. The 14th Amendment, ratified in 1868, guaranteed equal protection under the law to all citizens. The 15th Amendment, ratified in 1870, barred the federal and state governments from denying the right to vote to anyone "on account of race, color, or previous condition of servitude."

Once the North won the war, a major question was how to accept the Southern states back into the Union. Congress imposed a plan of "Reconstruction" on the defeated South. Individual Southern states could not be readmitted to the Union until they had written new constitutions ending slavery and extending equal rights to all citizens. African Americans rushed to exercise the rights long denied them. Thus, Blacks were elected to fill jobs on the local, state, and national levels. But this time of participation in the political process did not last long. By 1876, unapologetic Southern whites had regained control in all the Southern states. They passed laws that enforced segregation, or separation, of the races. Blacks lost most of the gains made during Reconstruction. It took until the middle of the 20th century for African Americans to begin to win back their full rights of citizenship. The struggle continues to this day.

# The Transcontinental Railroad

★ ★ ★ ★ ★

**By linking the regions of the nation, the social and economic life of Americans was transformed.**

### A New Area for Growth

In the early 1800s, the nation underwent a transportation revolution. New means of travel made communication and trade between distant regions of the nation much easier. Cities sprang up along the major routes, and the frontier moved westward.

On land, the National Road cut through the wilderness from Cumberland, Maryland, to Vandalia, Illinois. On water, the completion of the Erie Canal in 1825 started a boom in canal construction. At the same time, steamboats speeded travel on major rivers such as the Hudson and the Mississippi.

Steam-powered locomotives first appeared in the 1830s. By 1840, workers had laid three thousand miles of track. In 1849, the Pacific Railroad was the first to travel west of the Mississippi River. During the next decade, railroad construction continued with the help of grants of land from the federal government to the states and the railroad companies. But getting to California from the East still meant months of difficult travel by wagon or a long ocean voyage around the southernmost tip of South America—Cape Horn.

### Tracks Span the Continent

In the 1840s, a few American visionaries proposed a transcontinental railroad. Yet many doubted that such a railroad could be built. These doubters argued that the terrain was too rough and the cost too high.

People also disagreed about the best route. Not surprisingly, southerners favored a southern route, easterners a northern one, and westerners a central one. Finally in 1862, in the midst of the Civil War, President Lincoln and Congress made a decision. They chose the central route and chartered, or granted the right, to two companies to complete the job.

**The Big Race**   In 1863, the Union Pacific started building west from Omaha, Nebraska. At the same time, the Central Pacific pressed eastward from Sacramento, California. The

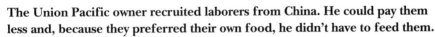

The Union Pacific owner recruited laborers from China. He could pay them less and, because they preferred their own food, he didn't have to feed them.

government helped both companies by giving them land and money. For each mile of track laid, a company would receive 40 square miles of land along the route. The companies could then sell this land to settlers. The government also lent money to the railroad companies based on the amount of track laid. Since the company that laid more track stood to gain more, the two companies entered into a fierce race.

The Union Pacific had the advantage of building over flat grasslands until it reached the Rocky Mountains. But its crews faced the threat of Indian attacks.

The Central Pacific had to get over the rugged Sierra Nevada Mountains before reaching the flatter lands that lay beyond. It drove its crews over the mountains in the middle of winter when several feet of snow might fall in a single day.

For this difficult and dangerous work, the company employed thousands of Chinese laborers. They dangled over the edges of cliffs in baskets to drill holes for blasting powder. They helped to drag locomotives over steep mountain passes. Hundreds lost their lives in the process.

**The Wedding of the Rails**  Six years after it began, this "work of giants" ended. With completion in sight, each company worked at a feverish pace. Union Pacific crews laid a record-breaking 8 miles of track in a single day. However, the Central Pacific's Chinese workers soon topped this record: they laid 10 miles of track in a day. When the final tally was in, the Union Pacific had laid 1,086 miles of track and the Central Pacific 689.

Leland Stanford, president of the Central Pacific, drove in the last spike—a golden one—joining the two lines at Promontory Point, Utah. The exciting news was telegraphed across the nation. East and West were now linked by rail. A journey that had once taken several months could now be made in a week!

Rail transportation in the United States today consists mainly of commuter and freight trains.

## Losses and Gains

The completion of the first transcontinental railroad was a remarkable achievement. But it had some negative effects. Construction crews and hunters had virtually destroyed the enormous herds of buffalo that had roamed the plains. The coming of the railroads also led to tragic wars with the Sioux Indians, who were angry about the loss of their land and the buffalo.

Over the next quarter century, four more transcontinental railroads were built. Thousands of Americans and immigrants from Europe came by rail to settle in the American West. They were drawn by the cheap land and the promise of a better life.

These new settlers no longer had to worry about being far from civilization. The same trains that carried them to the West now gave them access to factories in the East and markets for their produce. The rail network contributed to urban growth and the industrialization of the nation.

**Buffalo herds went from 13 million in the 1850s to near extinction by the 1890s. Without the buffalo, the Plains Indians couldn't survive.**

23

# The Pullman Strike

★ ★ ★ ★ ★

**The strike marked the first major confrontation between the federal government and the labor movement.**

**The power of the federal government was too great for the strikers.**

## Labor Unions Struggle

The rise of industry after the Civil War created problems for American workers. Many people worked long hours for low wages in large, dirty, and unsafe factories. During hard times, employers were likely to slash wages or, even worse, fire workers without warning. In an attempt to improve their lot, some workers formed unions.

These labor organizations tried to win higher wages, shorter hours, and better working conditions for their members. They did this through negotiations with employers, boycotts, and strikes. In the late 1800s, union efforts produced a series of violent clashes between workers and industrialists.

The first of these clashes occurred in 1877. A wage cut for workers on the Baltimore and Ohio Railroad resulted in a strike that spread to other railroads throughout the country:

- Violence erupted when state and federal troops fired on the strikers.

- Enraged workers destroyed millions of dollars' worth of property.

- One hundred people died.

In 1886, a strike at the McCormick Harvester plant in Chicago, Illinois, led to the Haymarket Riot. After several strikers were killed, some labor leaders organized a protest meeting at Haymarket Square. The police were called in to break up the meeting, and someone threw a bomb into the crowd. The riot that followed ended in tragedy:

- Seven people died.

- Seventy suffered injuries.

- Eight union leaders were arrested.

- Four union leaders were hanged.

Six years later, workers at the Homestead Steel plant in Pittsburgh, Pennsylvania, went on strike when their wages were cut. Determined to break the strike and crush the union, the plant manager, Henry Frick, who worked for steel manufacturer Andrew Carnegie, brought in 300 detectives. Armed strikers met them. A battle resulted:

- Nine strikers and seven guards died.

- Public opinion turned against the strikers when a radical agitator (who was not a union member) tried to assassinate Frick.

The strike ended in failure and the collapse of the union.

Debs had inspired thousands of railroad workers in 27 states to strike. Transportation from Chicago to the Pacific was at a complete standstill.

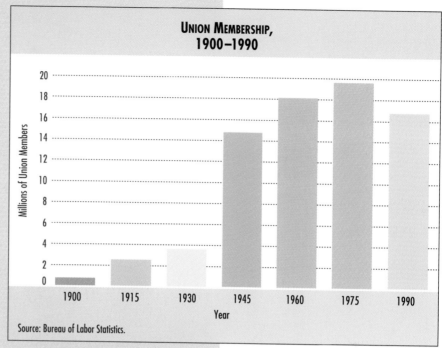

**UNION MEMBERSHIP, 1900–1990**

Millions of Union Members

1900 | 1915 | 1930 | 1945 | 1960 | 1975 | 1990

Year

Source: Bureau of Labor Statistics.

## Workers Strike the Pullman Plant

George Pullman considered himself a model employer. He owned a railroad sleeping car factory near Chicago, and he cared about his workers. He built a company town with houses, stores, parks, and a library for them. Then the depression of 1893 hit, and trouble followed.

Pullman cut his workers' wages several times. But he did not lower their rents or the prices they had to pay in the company stores.

**Debs Steps In** Most of the workers at the Pullman plant belonged to the newly formed American Railway Union. A fiery former railroad worker, Eugene V. Debs, headed the union. In 1894, when Pullman refused to negotiate with the workers over the wage cuts, the union called a strike. Unionized railroad workers throughout the country refused to move any train that had a Pullman car attached. By June, rail traffic west of Chicago had stopped.

**A Legal Weapon** Strikebreakers were brought in to replace the strik-

As unions achieved some successes, membership increased. The most impressive growth occured between 1930 and 1975. Membership declined somewhat in the 1980s due to an economic recession and high unemployment.

ing workers, and violence erupted. On July 2, a federal court issued an injunction, or court order, ordering the strikers to stop interfering with the trains. The court based its action on the Sherman Antitrust Act of 1890, which forbade the "restraint of trade or commerce." According to the court, the strikers were restraining, or holding back, interstate trade by interfering with mail delivery and the movement of goods by rail.

When railroad workers refused to obey the injunction, President Grover Cleveland sent two thousand federal troops to Chicago to break the strike. Eugene Debs was arrested for defying the injunction. The situation erupted into violence. Railroad property was destroyed, and 12 people died. By July 20, the strikers had given up and the union's power had been broken.

## Changes After the Pullman Strike

The Pullman strike convinced some people that American workers needed help. Progressive reformers pressed for laws to raise wages, shorten working hours, and improve working conditions. Some people decided that the American economic system itself needed to be changed radically. Debs, for example, emerged from jail and went on to found the Socialist Party of America in 1901. Most workers, however, continued to look to the unions to help them. During the decades that followed, union membership increased.

Nevertheless, unions remained too small to have much political influence. Also, management now had an effective new weapon—the court injunction. Companies used it repeatedly to end strikes.

Unions enjoyed some success, especially during World War I. But not until the 1930s did organized labor become strong enough to bring about lasting improvement in the lives of workers and their families.

# The Spanish-American War

★ ★ ★ ★ ★

The defeat of Spain marked the United States' arrival as a major world power.

This drawing, which appeared on the front page of a New York newspaper, increased war fever.

## Isolation Threatened

For most of the 19th century, the United States kept itself apart from the rest of the world. With the Monroe Doctrine in 1823, the United States warned European powers not to colonize or otherwise interfere in the affairs of the Western Hemisphere. When France took control of Mexico in the 1860s, the United States threatened to invade Mexico. But the French government soon toppled, and no further action was taken.

The United States had little interest in expansion in the 1860s and 1870s. The nation's energies and resources were spent on the Civil War and rebuilding the country afterward.

By the 1890s, however, a spirit of imperialism was emerging. This occurred for several reasons:

- The closing of the western frontier in the 1890s left the nation with little room for expansion.

- Trade in the Pacific—with China and Japan—had aroused American interest in the area.

- Americans were seeking new markets for the products of their expanding economy.

## Going to War with Spain

By the 1890s, the Caribbean island of Cuba was almost all that remained of Spain's former empire in the Americas. Unhappy with Spanish rule, the Cubans had revolted several times. They did so again in 1895. The Spanish lost no time in moving to crush this new uprising. The Spanish general, Valeriano Weyler (nicknamed "Butcher" Weyler by the American press), rounded up thousands of Cubans and forced them into concentration camps. Many died there of disease and malnutrition.

Eager to increase the sales of their newspapers, several publishers ran exaggerated accounts of Spanish brutality. This "yellow journalism," in such newspapers as William Randolph Hearst's *New York World* and Joseph Pulitzer's *New York Journal,* sparked a public outcry for U.S. intervention on behalf of the Cubans. Still,

the American government tried to resolve matters through diplomacy. Then a startling event occurred that pushed the nation over the brink into a war.

**"Remember the *Maine*"** On February 15, 1898, a gigantic explosion ripped through the U.S. battleship *Maine* while it lay at anchor in Havana harbor. The explosion destroyed the ship and killed more than 200 crew members. The explosion was probably caused by a mechanical malfunction on the ship. But outraged Americans blamed it on Spain.

The sinking of the *Maine* gave an excuse to those who had long been spoiling for a fight. One of these people was Theodore Roosevelt, the assistant secretary of the navy. Rallying with the cry "Remember the *Maine!*" Roosevelt and others forced President William McKinley to declare war on

Dewey's swift defeat of the Spanish fleet removed competition in the Pacific and led to U.S. influence in the Philippines.

This cartoon, from a British magazine, shows America trying out its new role as a world power after the victory over Spain.

Spain. While voting for war, in April 1898, Congress adopted a resolution known as the Teller Amendment. It stated that the United States had no plans to annex Cuba.

**"Splendid Little War"** The Spanish-American War began with a big victory for the United States. The American naval commander, George Dewey, had orders to attack the Spanish fleet in the Philippine Islands in the event of war. Less than two weeks after the declaration of war, the new steel battleships under Dewey's command steamed into Manila Bay. They wiped out the Spanish fleet there. Dewey's victory shattered Spanish naval power in the Pacific. Unlike the U.S. Navy, which had been modernized in the 1880s and 1890s, the U.S. Army was ill prepared and ill equipped. It took two months to train the thousands of volunteers who signed up. Resigning his post with the

navy, Roosevelt organized a cavalry regiment of college athletes, cowboys, and Native Americans. He called them the Rough Riders.

In June, the Rough Riders heroically stormed and captured Kettle Hill outside the port city of Santiago, Cuba. The fighting in Cuba ended after American ships destroyed another Spanish fleet, this one in Santiago harbor. American troops in Puerto Rico and the Philippines won quick victories, too.

In all, the Spanish-American War lasted only ten weeks and cost the United States only a few hundred lives in actual combat. (Thousands of American soldiers died of disease, however.) Secretary of State John Hay referred to the conflict as "a splendid little war."

## An Empire in the Pacific

Spain and the United States signed the Treaty of Paris in 1898. Cuba won its independence, but under terms favorable to the United States. The United States had the right to intervene in Cuban affairs and to maintain naval and coaling stations on the island. The treaty also gave the United States possession of Puerto Rico, Guam, and the Philippines, for which it paid Spain $20 million. The acquisition of the Philippines involved the United States in a brutal war to defeat Filipino rebels fighting for their country's independence.

With a Pacific empire, the United States became more interested in East Asia. In 1898 and 1899, it adopted the "open door policy" to keep China open to European, Japanese, and American merchants. In 1900, it joined the European powers in putting down a rebellion in China against Western influence.

# The Treaty of Versailles

★ ★ ★ ★ ★

**The treaty ended the First World War and set the conditions that led to the Second.**

## World War I

When war broke out in Europe in 1914, President Woodrow Wilson worked hard to keep the United States out of the fighting. The war pitted the Central Powers (Germany and Austria-Hungary) against the Allies (Britain, France, Italy, and Russia). Wilson urged both sides to negotiate a "peace without victory."

Although Wilson insisted that America was neutral, American bankers and industrialists were lending the Allies money and shipping them supplies. To disrupt this aid, Germany launched a silent, deadly submarine war against the Allies, and Americans traveling on Allied ships were killed. The United States found it increasingly difficult to remain neutral. Finally, in April 1917, the nation declared war on Germany.

That same spring, a revolution brought the Bolsheviks to power in Russia, and the new government withdrew from the war. German armies could now concentrate on fighting Britain and France, which were tired from years of war. American help came in the nick of time.

In January 1918, with the war still raging, Wilson issued his "Fourteen Points" to be used in planning the peace settlement. They included disarmament, free trade, freedom of the seas, self-determination of nations, an end to secret diplomacy, and a League of Nations to settle international disputes and prevent future wars.

## America "Loses" the Peace

On November 11, 1918, Germany and the Allies signed the armistice that stopped the fighting. Germany hoped for a peace based on Wilson's Fourteen Points.

**A Harsh Peace** In January 1919, delegates from many nations gathered in Paris at the Palace of Versailles for the peace conference. Instead of sending a delegate to represent the United States, Wilson attended the conference himself. In France, cheering crowds hailed him as the great peacemaker.

The Allied nations dominated the talks. In addition to Wilson, the "Big Four" included Georges Clemenceau of France, David Lloyd George of Britain, and Vittorio Orlando of Italy. All three were practical politicians. They regarded Wilson's Fourteen Points as useful propaganda but planned to follow their own national interests. France especially wanted to weaken Germany so that it could never threaten Europe again. Britain also believed that Germany deserved punishment. Italy wanted as much new territory as it could get.

Wilson realized that he would have to compromise to achieve his major goal—the League of Nations. The points he compromised included freedom of the seas, free trade, and the idea of a peace that would not punish Germany. Wilson also had to compromise on the principle of national self-determination. For example, Italy had gained new territory inhabited

**Fresh troops from the United States helped to end years of stalemate on the battlefield and to ensure Allied victory in World War I.**

mostly by Austrians, who would now be under Italian rule.

Nevertheless, Wilson won an important victory in getting the charter for the League of Nations included in the treaty. He was convinced that the League would later be able to correct any mistakes or unfairness in the treaty.

On June 28, 1919, after strong protests and with much reluctance, Germany signed the treaty. The final terms of the treaty forced Germany to admit responsibility for starting the war. Germany also lost valuable territory. Alsace-Lorraine went back to France. Several German-speaking areas became part of Poland and Czechoslovakia. The treaty stripped Germany of its overseas colonies, reduced its armed forces, and imposed large payments of damages to the nations it had fought. Wilson called the treaty a "very severe settlement."

**The Fight for Ratification** When he returned to the United States, Wilson met mounting opposition to the treaty in the Senate, and especially to the League. Some senators were angry because they had not been included in the peace talks. Others wanted to change the treaty to ensure that the League would not commit American troops to war without congressional approval. And some, fearful of U.S. entanglement in foreign conflicts, refused to accept the League under any circumstances.

In September 1919, Wilson took his case to the people. He embarked on a nationwide speaking tour to promote the League. Although the crowds responded with enthusiasm, the trip tired the President. Forced to return to Washington, D.C., Wilson suffered a stroke that left him paralyzed on one side, and even more unwilling to compromise on the League.

The harshness of the treaty helped to create the conditions that led to Hitler's rise to power—and an even bloodier world war.

## After the Treaty

The Senate did not ratify the Treaty of Versailles. In 1921, the United States signed a separate peace treaty with Germany. The United States did not join the League of Nations, preferring to avoid involvement in foreign countries. Despite this generally isolationist attitude, the United States participated in several international conferences aimed at promoting peace.

Germany had emerged from the war humiliated by defeat and burdened by its huge payments. Germany's new democratic government had a shaky beginning amid runaway inflation. In addition, the government proved unable to improve conditions during the worldwide depression that followed. Under these desperate economic conditions, Adolf Hitler's Nazi Party gained power. His appeal was largely based on a call to right the wrongs of the Versailles Treaty. Ultimately, Hitler's actions led to another world war.

**Wilson brought new ideas of what peace should be. The other leaders, however, saw a need to achieve nationalistic political gains rather than support Wilson's idealistic goals.**

# National Origins Act, 1924

★ ★ ★ ★ ★

**The passage of this legislation closed America's open door to immigrants.**

## Rolling Up the Welcome Mat

For the first hundred years of its history, the United States welcomed most immigrants with open arms. Many of these immigrants came from the British Isles and northern Europe. They left their countries to escape religious and political oppression and poverty. In America, they filled a growing demand for laborers.

After 1890, however, the pattern of immigrations changed. Large numbers of immigrants from eastern and southern Europe arrived on American shores. Protestant Americans regarded these new immigrants with suspicion and fear, since many were either Catholic or Jewish. Native-born American workers resented the immigrants who were willing to work for less. They feared that these new immigrants would bring down wages and cost the Americans their jobs.

On the West Coast, strong feeling against Asian immigrants led to the passage of the Chinese Exclusion Act of 1882. This first law to restrict immigration barred Chinese workers from entering the United States. Then, in an agreement with Japan in 1907, the United States limited the number of Japanese who could enter the country.

During World War I, the volume of immigration dropped sharply. But when the war ended, it began to rise again. Those immigrants who came in the 1920s found that they were much less welcome than those who had preceded them.

## America Shuts the Door

**A Time of Intolerance** Antiforeign feeling had always existed in America to some degree. But during the 1920s, it reached new heights. World War I had caused a burst of nationalism and patriotic feeling. Many immigrants, especially those from Germany, were hated because they were thought to be more loyal to their homelands than to America. Moreover, many immigrants were suspected of being politically radical or revolutionary.

In Russia, the Bolsheviks had seized power in 1917 and had established a Communist government. Rumors of "Red" revolutions erupting in Europe raised the level of anxiety in America. Immigrants were thought to be the instigators of revolution in the United States.

▼ Hundreds of thousands of immigrants sought a better life in the United States. But they were regarded with suspicion by those who had preceded them.

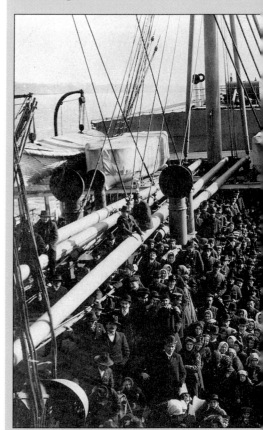

| IMMIGRATION TO THE UNITED STATES, 1880–1930 | | | | | | |
|---|---|---|---|---|---|---|
| | 1880 | 1890 | 1900 | 1910 | 1920 | 1930 |
| Great Britain | 73,273 | 69,730 | 12,509 | 68,941 | 38,471 | 31,015 |
| Ireland | 71,603 | 53,024 | 35,730 | 29,855 | 9,591 | 23,445 |
| Central Europe (Germany, Poland) | 104,082 | 159,699 | 133,354 | 290,020 | 11,480 | 44,984 |
| Eastern Europe (USSR, Baltic states) | 5,049 | 36,321 | 97,639 | 212,079 | 5,664 | 4,931 |
| Southern Europe (Italy, Spain, Greece, Portugal) | 13,985 | 55,963 | 108,495 | 254,277 | 143,154 | 26,974 |
| Asia (Japan, China, Philippines) | 5,839 | 4,448 | 17,946 | 23,533 | 17,505 | 4,535 |

Source: U.S. Bureau of the Census, *Historical Statistics of the United States—Colonial Times to 1970.*

After the war, Socialists and Communists were blamed for a series of crippling strikes and bombing incidents that swept across the nation. These incidents resulted in the so-called Red Scare of 1919. Thousands of radicals, including many immigrants, were rounded up and thrown into jail in violation of their civil liberties. Although the Red Scare didn't last long, the intense dislike of radicals continued. This ill feeling expanded to include most foreigners as well. In 1927, two Italian immigrants—Nicola Sacco and Bartolomeo Vanzetti—were accused of robbery and murder and were executed. Although the evidence presented at their trial was questionable, both men held radical political views. They were, therefore, presumed to be guilty.

The revival of the Ku Klux Klan was further evidence of the antiforeigner feeling of the 1920s. White Southerners founded the Klan after the Civil War. Originally an antiblack organization, the Klan now made targets of immigrants, Jews, and Catholics—in short, anyone who was the least bit different from Protestant, native-born Americans.

**Setting Quotas** In 1921, Congress passed a law that introduced the quota system to the immigration process. The new law limited immigration to three percent of the number of people of each nationality living in the United States in 1910.

Three years later, Congress passed the National Origins Act of 1924. This new law established even stricter quotas. Each country's quota was cut back to two percent, and the base year was moved back to 1890. Most immigrants who had come to the United States before the 1890s were from the British Isles and northwestern Europe. Thus the new law severely reduced the number of immigrants allowed from southern and eastern Europe. The National Origins Act totally barred immigration from China and Japan.

## Immigration After 1924

As some of its supporters had hoped, the new law did reduce competition for jobs. Nevertheless, further restrictions were placed on immigration in 1929 and again in 1931. During the Great Depression of the 1930s, immigration did not exceed 100,000 in any one year. Immigration rates also stayed low during World War II.

With a few changes, the National Origins Act remained in effect for 40 years. One change came in 1952, when the ban against Asian peoples was lifted.

By the 1960s, many Americans had become convinced of the need for immigration reform. In 1965, Congress passed a new law eliminating quotas based on national origin. The law permitted 170,000 people from the Eastern Hemisphere and 120,000 from the Western Hemisphere to enter the United States every year. Close relatives of people already living in the United States were exempt from these quotas. The 1965 law brought a surge of immigrants from Asia, the West Indies, and Latin America, which continues to the present. Like those who came before them, most of these new immigrants were escaping war, famine, and political turmoil in their countries.

▼ **This political cartoon suggests that many of those who opposed immigration were once immigrants themselves.**

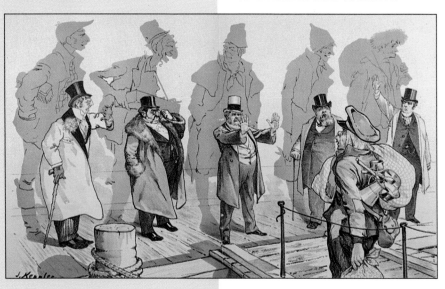

# The Great Depression
★ ★ ★ ★ ★

A devastating economic crisis left millions of Americans without jobs, homes, or food.

## Buying and Borrowing

The 1920s were a period of great prosperity. More Americans than ever before seemed to have money to spend on luxury items, such as automobiles, radios, and refrigerators. Yet not everyone shared in the good times.

Industrial wages rose slowly, and farm prices remained low. Thus many factory workers and farmers could not afford to buy the new products that were being manufactured. With sales lagging behind production, key industries—such as automobiles and home construction—slumped.

Many Americans stretched their incomes by borrowing. They bought large, expensive items on credit and obtained mortgages to purchase homes. Many investors bought stock, or shares in a company, "on margin." They paid for only part of the stock's value and borrowed the rest from their stockbroker, or trader.

In the 1920s, heavy investment in the stock market sent prices of shares soaring. But on October 29, 1929, the market crashed. Fearing an end to the boom, investors panicked and rushed to sell their shares. Prices plummeted, wiping out the life savings of many people.

The Depression hit people of all types—urban, rural, white, black, working-class, middle-class. One year, unemployment hit one in every four workers.

## A Depression Grips the Nation

The stock market crash did not cause the Great Depression. But it set off a chain reaction that plunged the nation into the worst period of hard times it had ever known.

To cover their losses in the stock market, many investors withdrew their money from the banks. Other people took the money from their savings to pay their mortgages and other bills. Soon the steady movement of people withdrawing their money from the banks became a "run." With their funds used up, many banks closed their doors. By 1933, two-thirds of the nation's banks had failed.

Lacking both money and customers, thousands of businesses shut down. And millions of workers lost their jobs. In the early 1930s, about 12 million people—25 percent of the workforce—were unemployed. Many Americans were forced to take

As the economy collapsed, shantytowns sprang up across the country. This "Hooverville" was in Seattle, Washington.

| BANK FAILURES, BUSINESS FAILURES, AND UNEMPLOYMENT DURING THE GREAT DEPRESSION | | | |
|---|---|---|---|
| | Bank Failures | Business Failures | Unemployment (in thousands) |
| 1930 | 1,352 | 26,355 | 4,340 |
| 1932 | 1,456 | 31,822 | 12,060 |
| 1934 | | 12,091 | 11,340 |
| 1936 | | 9,607 | 9,030 |
| 1938 | | 12,836 | 10,390 |
| 1940 | 448 | 13,619 | 8,120 |

The unprecedented number of bank failures caused the closing of many businesses. This, in turn, resulted in record numbers of unemployed workers. Roosevelt's New Deal programs put people back to work and helped the nation get through the hard times.

any job they could get. Some sold apples or pencils on city streets. Others roamed the country looking for work. Nearly 2 million young men became hoboes, "riding the rails" from city to city.

Without work or savings, many people lost their homes when they failed to make their mortgage payments or pay their rent. The growing number of homeless people built communities of shacks on the edges of cities. They named these neighborhoods "Hoovervilles" after President Herbert Hoover.

Unemployment also meant that people had no money to buy food. They scrounged in garbage cans for scraps, sent their children begging, or stood for hours in breadlines that stretched for blocks. Countless Americans suffered; some died of malnutrition and starvation.

Farmers fared even worse than city dwellers. As farm prices fell, many farmers went into debt. An estimated one-third of all American farmers lost their farms.

**The Dust Bowl** In the early 1930s, a long period of drought deepened the misery of farmers on the Great Plains. The prolonged dry spell produced huge clouds of dust that swept across the plains. They buried equipment, livestock, and farmhouses. What had once been fertile farmland was transformed into an arid desert. Some 400,000 people abandoned their farms and headed west, joining hordes of others uprooted by the Great Depression.

**President Hoover's Response** In the beginning, President Hoover believed the Depression would end soon. He repeatedly told Americans that prosperity was "just around the corner." Not until 1932 did Hoover try to relieve the suffering and despair.

The President asked Congress for millions of dollars to provide jobs building schools, roads, and bridges. He also established a special government agency to lend money to banks, city and state governments, and some large businesses to keep them operating.

But Hoover stopped short of providing direct federal relief to the needy. He felt that to do so would undermine the American tradition of individual self-help. And when nearly 15,000 unemployed World War I veterans marched on the capital to demand payment of the bonuses due them, Hoover had them forcibly removed by the army.

## Help Arrives: A New Deal

In 1932, Franklin Delano Roosevelt won the presidency on a pledge to give depression-stricken Americans a "New Deal." Unlike Hoover, Roosevelt was willing to try anything that might help. "The only thing we have to fear is fear itself," he declared.

During the first hundred days of Roosevelt's administration, Congress passed legislation to rescue banks, help farmers, create a job corps, and work with businesses to raise wages and create new jobs. Later New Deal reforms included Social Security to provide income for retired people and unemployed workers. Millions of Americans still benefit from programs, such as Social Security, that were created during the Depression.

Although New Deal programs helped relieve the worst of the suffering, the nation did not fully recover from the Great Depression until World War II. The New Deal also greatly expanded the power of the presidency and of government in general. For the first time in the nation's history, the federal government assumed responsibility for the economic and social welfare of its citizens.

# The Attack on Pearl Harbor

★ ★ ★ ★ ★

A surprise Japanese attack brought the United States into a second world war.

## War in Europe

In 1939, 20 years after World War I, Americans again heard ominous news from Europe. The Nazi invasion of Poland had provoked Britain and France to declare war on Germany and Italy, beginning World War II. Although the United States had declared itself neutral, President Franklin Roosevelt created a "lend-lease" system to help the Allies. This plan allowed the President to sell, lend, or lease arms to any nation considered vital to the defense of the United States. When Germany invaded the Soviet Union in June 1941, lend-lease was extended to the Soviet Union.

In the Pacific, relations between the United States and Japan became strained over the issue of China. Despite warnings from the United States, Japan continued to assault China. The United States then refused to sell needed raw materials to Japan. In September 1940, Japan signed a defensive agreement with Germany and Italy. The three were called the Axis powers.

## The Attack on Pearl Harbor

Although America's attention was focused on the war in Europe, the nation's entry into the conflict occurred on the other side of the world—in the Pacific. The United States and Japan held peace talks, but accomplished nothing. Then on November 26, 1941, a Japanese fleet set out in secret toward Pearl Harbor, the main U.S. naval base in the Pacific. A few days later, the commander of the Japanese fleet received the coded message "Climb Mount Nitaka," which meant "Attack Pearl Harbor." And they did.

At 7:55 A.M. on December 7, 1941, Japanese planes bombed the U.S. naval base at Pearl Harbor in Hawaii, shattering the Sunday morning stillness. The attack caught the base completely by surprise. Torpedo hits shot great columns of water into the air. In a matter of minutes, the harbor was engulfed in thick smoke from the burning oil.

The attack lasted less than two hours, but the damage to the U.S. Pacific fleet was enormous.

- More than a dozen battleships and cruisers were sunk or badly damaged.
- Over 180 aircraft were destroyed.
- More than 2,000 Americans were killed.

Nearly half of the casualties occurred when the battleship *Arizona* blew up. Japan lost only 29 planes and 3 submarines.

The Japanese attack on Pearl Harbor outraged the American people. Referring to December 7 as "a date which will live in infamy," President Roosevelt asked Congress for a declaration of war against Japan. Only one person voted against the declaration.

**A Japanese plane prepares to leave a carrier's deck for the attack on Pearl Harbor. Thorough planning by the Japanese high command contributed to the success of the surprise attack.**

This World War II poster encouraged women to join the war effort—and they did. In large numbers, women filled the jobs as men went off to fight.

By dropping atomic bombs on two Japanese cities, the United States ended the war. But the bombing also began an age in which people feared the total destruction of the earth.

## World War II

Preparing to fight a global war required a massive effort, and life in the United States was greatly altered. With so many men in the armed forces, women had to fill jobs as railroad workers, shipbuilders, and aircraft riveters. Raw materials needed for the war effort, such as gasoline, cloth, sugar, and meat, were in short supply and had to be rationed.

Sadly, life was most greatly altered for Japanese Americans. Fearing that these people posed a threat to national security, the government forced about 110,000 Japanese Americans to live in detention camps during the war.

**War in Europe** As America was gearing up for the fight, the Axis powers—Germany, Italy, and Japan—were seizing even more territory. Allied leaders decided to focus the war effort first on Europe, then on Japan. The United States and Britain conducted a series of air attacks that weakened the centers of German war production and communications. The defeat of German forces in North Africa in 1943 allowed the Allies to advance to the Italian mainland, and the Italian government soon surrendered. On June 6, 1944, called D-Day, General Dwight D. Eisenhower successfully landed a huge invasion force along the coast of Normandy in France. For the next year, the Allied army pushed east toward Germany, liberating towns from Nazi control along the way. Meanwhile, troops from the Soviet Union, fighting with the Allies, pressured Germany from the opposite direction. German troops rallied for a time, but finally—exhausted and demoralized—Germany surrendered on May 7, 1945.

**War in the Far East** As the Allies gained the upper hand in Europe, the United States focused more attention on the war in the Pacific. After winning naval battles in the Coral Sea and at Midway Island in 1942, American forces embarked on a strategy of air strikes. The Japanese were fierce fighters, but by 1945 the United States had won back the Philippines and many other islands. Victories at Iwo Jima and Okinawa brought the United States almost to Japan's doorstep. The next step seemed to be an invasion of Japan. But American leaders feared that such an attack would kill hundreds of thousands of Americans. Harry Truman, now President after Roosevelt's death in 1945, decided to use a secret weapon. He authorized the dropping of atomic bombs on two Japanese cities—Hiroshima on August 6 and Nagasaki on August 9. The bombs caused untold death and suffering. Japan surrendered on August 14, 1945.

# Montgomery Bus Boycott

★ ★ ★ ★ ★

**By capturing the nation's attention, this protest set the civil rights movement in motion.**

**Strong organization and complete dedication helped Montgomery's black community maintain its boycott for over a year.**

## A Segregated Society

FOR WHITES ONLY! This sign was posted on public facilities throughout the segregated South of the 1950s—on restroom doors, drinking fountains, and at department store lunch counters. Black people who wished to use a public drinking fountain had to find one marked FOR COLORED PEOPLE.

In this segregated society, Blacks and whites lived in different neighborhoods, attended separate schools, used separate recreational facilities, and sat in separate sections on city buses. Segregation in the South was enforced by local and state laws. If a black person crossed the color line in a store, restaurant, or hotel, he or she could be arrested. Segregation denied black people their civil rights and made them second-class citizens.

In 1954, the United States Supreme Court, in the case of *Brown* v. *Topeka Board of Education,* declared that separate educational facilities could not be equal and that they denied citizens their rights to equal protection of the law. This landmark decision gave black Americans hope that the federal government would put an end to segregation.

## A Long Year of Protest

On the evening of December 1, 1955, Mrs. Rosa Parks, an African American, boarded a bus in Montgomery, Alabama. She dutifully took a seat toward the middle of the bus but still in the black section. When the white section of the bus filled up, the bus driver asked her to give up her seat for a white male passenger. Mrs. Parks was tired after a long day at work, and, as she later said, "I felt that I had a right to be treated as any other passenger." Rosa Parks spoke a simple word that launched amazing changes. She said, "No."

When Rosa Parks was arrested, outraged black citizens of Montgomery formed a group to protest.

They chose Martin Luther King, Jr., a young minister, to lead them in a boycott of Montgomery's transit system. Nearly all of Montgomery's 50,000 African Americans refused to ride city buses. They walked to work or to school. They formed car pools. Their boycott went on for over a year, and during that time the Montgomery bus company nearly went broke.

In June 1956, a federal court ruled that segregated seating violated the United States Constitution. The city of Montgomery appealed, but the Supreme Court upheld the decision. Montgomery's buses were desegregated in December 1956, and the boycott ended.

## Leading to Legislation

The success of the Montgomery bus boycott led to demonstrations, marches, and more boycotts throughout the South to protest racial injustice. Many African Americans deliberately set out to defy local segregation laws. One tactic they used was the sit-in: they sat at "whites only" lunch counters until they were dragged away by the police. After one group of protesters was arrested, another group took its place. Another tactic was freedom rides. Black and white college students rode interstate buses. These "freedom riders" deliberately tried to use white restrooms, register in white hotels, and eat in white restaurants.

The civil rights movement encountered much violence, including the death of several civil rights workers. In 1957, violence threatened to erupt in Little Rock, Arkansas, when nine black students tried to enroll at Central High School. Arkansas governor Orval Faubus called up the National Guard to prevent the students from entering. President Dwight Eisenhower "federalized" the Guard, ordering them to protect the black students and enforce the Supreme Court's order to integrate the school. After a time, however, the civil rights movement began to achieve considerable success. Communities began to change their laws. Congress acted, too, passing civil rights legislation in 1957 and 1960, which called for ending segregation of hotels, restaurants, and other public accommodations.

The Montgomery bus boycott also elevated Martin Luther King, Jr., to national prominence. He continued to organize boycotts, sit-ins, marches, and rallies in other parts of the South. An eloquent speaker, Dr. King inspired many people, black and white, to support the civil rights movement. Following the teachings of Mohandas Gandhi, King, in turn, encouraged his followers to react nonviolently when they were heckled, spat on, and even beaten by white segregationists. The use of passive resistance gained much respect for the movement.

The climax of the civil rights movement came on August 28, 1963, when Dr. King led more than 200,000 people in a march on Washington, D.C., to demand "jobs and freedom" for all American citizens. On the steps of the Lincoln Memorial, Dr. King delivered his powerful "I have a dream" speech in which he envisioned a day when all people would join hands in peace. A short time later, Congress passed major legislation—the Civil Rights Act of 1964 and the Voting Rights Act of 1965—that prohibited discrimination on the basis of race, creed, or gender.

### Milestones of the Civil Rights Movement

**1954** Supreme Court declares segregation in public schools unconstitutional.

**1955** Montgomery, Alabama: Blacks begin a year-long boycott of city buses after Rosa Parks's arrest.

**1957** Little Rock, Arkansas: nine black students try to desegregate Central High School.

**1960** Greensboro, North Carolina: first lunch counter sit-in.

**1962** James Meredith becomes first African American student to enroll at the University of Mississippi.

**1964** Congress passes Civil Rights Act.

**1965** Congress passes Voting Rights Act.

**1968** Assassination of Martin Luther King, Jr.

**1969** Shirley Chisholm (New York) becomes nation's first black woman elected to U.S. House of Representatives.

**1972** Congress passes Equal Opportunity Employment Act.

**1986** The United States officially observes Martin Luther King Day.

**1989** L. Douglas Wilder (Virginia) becomes the nation's first African American governor.

**1992** Carol Moseley Braun (Illinois) becomes the nation's first African American woman senator.

King's leadership and the power of his words inspired millions to support the civil rights movement.

# The Cuban Missile Crisis

★ ★ ★ ★ ★

**A confrontation with the Soviet Union threatened to turn the Cold War into nuclear war.**

## The Cold War Close to Home

Following World War II, the United States and the Soviet Union were locked in the icy grip of a Cold War. The United States tried to stop what it saw as efforts to spread communism to the rest of the world. The two superpowers constantly tried to frighten each other with their arsenals of nuclear weapons.

At the same time, rebels in Asian, African, and Latin American countries were trying to take control of their governments from dictators and foreign rulers. One of those countries was Cuba. From 1933 to 1958, Cuba was ruled by Fulgencio Batista, a corrupt dictator who had close ties to the United States. Over the years, opposition to Batista grew. Then in 1959, Fidel Castro overthrew the dictator. Angry over what he saw as decades of American control of Cuba, Castro seized foreign-owned businesses. In response, the United States reduced the amount of sugar—Cuba's chief export—it bought from the island nation. Finally the United States broke off diplomatic relations with Cuba in January 1961.

Castro began to refer to himself as a Communist. Furthermore, he was receiving more and more aid from the Soviet Union. Many in the United States feared what might happen with a Communist nation only 90 miles from Florida.

**Bay of Pigs** Convinced that Cuba posed a threat, the U.S. government decided to overthrow Castro. The Central Intelligence Agency (CIA) secretly organized, trained, and equipped a small army of anti-Castro Cuban exiles. Although the project had been started during President Eisenhower's administration, it was President John F. Kennedy who authorized the attack.

Before dawn on April 17, 1961, approximately 1,500 armed exiles landed at the Bay of Pigs on Cuba's southern coast. They expected coverage by American air and naval artillery. They also expected that thousands within Cuba would meet them and help topple Castro. Instead, the exiles were left stranded. Within two days, well-armed Castro forces had captured all the invaders.

The fiasco of the Bay of Pigs struck a serious blow to U.S. prestige and greatly embarrassed President Kennedy. Not only Communist countries but neutral nations and even U.S. allies condemned the action. Now Castro had even more reason to strengthen ties with the Soviet Union. Cuba became an even greater threat to the United States.

**The Cuban Missile Crisis brought the world to the brink of nuclear war. The fate of the world rested in large part in the hands of President Kennedy and his advisers.**

This cartoonist compared the Cuban Missile Crisis to a showdown in the Old West. Fortunately, the shooting never started.

U.S. vessels accompanied Soviet ships, ready to board on White House orders to look for missiles.

## The October Confrontation

The Bay of Pigs invasion gave Soviet premier Nikita Khrushchev an excuse to move "defensive" weapons into Cuba. During the summer of 1962, U.S. intelligence agents discovered that Soviet ships were bringing military equipment and thousands of Soviet technicians into Cuba. They suspected that the Soviets were building sites for guided missiles. Aerial photographs taken by spy planes on October 14 confirmed this suspicion.

President Kennedy considered the building of missile sites an appalling act of aggression. They placed nuclear weapons within range to destroy many American cities. But his choices were difficult. If he tried to negotiate with the Soviets, they would gain time to complete the missile sites. If he ordered U.S. forces to invade Cuba, he risked starting World War III.

On October 22, President Kennedy addressed the nation on television and revealed the news. He announced that he was authorizing a naval and air blockade around Cuba. All Soviet ships headed for the island would be stopped and searched for offensive weapons. He also demanded that the Soviet Union dismantle the missile bases and remove all weapons capable of striking the United States. If the Soviets did not comply with these demands, they could expect a "full retaliatory response."

The crisis brought the world to the brink of nuclear war. For nearly a week, people everywhere held their breath, waiting to see what the Soviets would do. Work on the missile sites speeded up for a few days. Then, suddenly, Khrushchev backed down. He agreed to withdraw the missiles in exchange for a U.S. pledge not to invade Cuba. On October 27, the crisis ended.

## Moving Toward Cooperation

The Cuban Missile Crisis was the most direct and dangerous confrontation of the Cold War. The outcome was considered a victory for the United States.

Rather than heightening tension between the rival superpowers, the showdown actually decreased hostilities. Both countries had been shaken by the events of October 1962. They realized how horrible a nuclear war would be. One sign of the reduced antagonism was the installation of a "hot line." This telephone system connected the President to the Soviet premier so that they could have immediate and direct talks in the event of a future crisis. Another sign was a treaty. In July 1963, both nations agreed to ban tests of nuclear weapons in the atmosphere. This was the first step toward reducing nuclear arms. The two nations continued to talk about limiting nuclear arms. However, with the breakup of the Soviet Union in 1991, the future of the talks remains uncertain.

# The Vietnam War

★ ★ ★ ★ ★

A long and bloody war divided the American people and helped create a generation that mistrusted the government.

## Containing Communism

During the Cold War, the United States government pursued a policy of containing communism wherever it spread. One of those spots was Vietnam, part of a former French colony in Southeast Asia. After years of fighting, Vietnamese rebels won their independence in 1954. Vietnam was divided into two territories, a Communist North Vietnam and a pro-Western South Vietnam. Elections to unite the country were scheduled, but they never occurred.

Communist guerrillas, known as the Vietcong and aided by North Vietnam, tried to overthrow the government of South Vietnam. In 1956, President Dwight Eisenhower dispatched 700 military advisers to South Vietnam. As the civil war intensified, President John Kennedy increased the number of advisers to 16,000.

## War Divides the Nation

**Gulf of Tonkin Resolution** In August 1964, President Lyndon Johnson announced that North Vietnamese gunboats had torpedoed two American destroyers in the Gulf of Tonkin. Seeing this as a clear act of aggression, Congress passed the Gulf of Tonkin Resolution. It gave the President almost unlimited power to use military force to retaliate.

Johnson rapidly escalated the war. From the end of 1965 to the middle of 1968, the number of American soldiers in Vietnam climbed from 184,000 to 538,000. U.S. planes began bombing strategic sites in North Vietnam. The United States was involved in a full-scale, but undeclared, war. Many people in the United States opposed that war. They protested in mass marches or by refusing to be drafted into the armed services.

Despite having huge numbers of men and powerful weapons, the United States had difficulty with the enemy. North Vietnam fought a guerrilla war of hit and run. Still, U.S. commanders clung to the mistaken belief that more troops and stronger weapons would gradually wear down the enemy.

**Tet Offensive** After months of stalemate, with neither side making progress, the war broke wide open. Beginning on January 30, 1968—which was Tet, a national holiday—the North Vietnamese launched a massive surprise attack on major cities in South Vietnam, including the capital, Saigon.

The Communists failed to overthrow the South Vietnamese and suffered enormous casualties. But the Tet Offensive weakened support for

U.S. general William Westmoreland (*center*) is shown here with American and South Vietnamese military personnel. The United States played a major role in the war from the mid-1960s to the early 1970s. As South Vietnamese troops took over the fighting, U.S. troops withdrew.

the war in the United States. Newspaper and television reports of the Tet Offensive revealed savage fighting and the fierce determination of the Communists to win no matter what the cost. Many more Americans began to doubt U.S. ability to win the war.

In the months following the Tet Offensive, the movement in the United States against the war grew quickly and steadily. Demonstrations—sometimes turning violent—took place on over 400 college campuses. Congress became bitterly divided between "hawks"—those defending the war—and "doves"—those opposing the war. Public opposition became so widespread that by the spring of 1968 President Johnson decided not to seek reelection.

**Vietnamization** Richard Nixon won the presidency in 1968. Although he promised to wind down the war, the fighting continued for four more years. Peace talks with North Vietnam began, but they seemed to go nowhere. President Nixon began a policy called Vietnamization. In this plan, South Vietnamese troops would gradually take over most of the fighting, allowing U.S. troops to withdraw. Hoping to strengthen South Vietnam's bargaining position at the peace talks, Nixon ordered the heaviest and most destructive bombings of the entire war. This set off another round of antiwar demonstrations in the United States. Finally, in January 1973, a cease-fire agreement was signed. It lasted just long enough for most of the U.S. troops to be evacuated from Vietnam.

As the Communists approached Saigon, the capital of South Vietnam, desperate South Vietnamese tried to board U.S. evacuation helicopters.

## The Casualties of War

Shortly after the Americans withdrew, fighting resumed. Without U.S. military support, the South Vietnamese were defeated in 1975. Vietnam became one country again. More than 1.2 million Vietnamese soldiers had died in combat and countless civilians had been killed. A beautiful country had been devastated by years of bombing and chemical warfare.

The long, bloody war was destructive for the United States as well. More than 58,000 young men and women were killed or missing in action. The Vietnam War had tremendous social, economic, and political costs. "Doves" lost faith in their government and began to distrust their leaders. "Hawks" blamed biased news media and a fainthearted Democratic Party for preventing an American military victory. The divisions between hawks and doves persisted for 20 years after the war's conclusion. To pay the high cost of the war, the government had gone deeper into debt, hurting the economy. The experience of the Vietnam War eroded the nation's confidence in its ability to create a just society at home and maintain peace abroad.

**Many Vietnam veterans, emotionally and physically scarred by their experience, joined the movement against the war.**

# The Reagan Election
★ ★ ★ ★ ★

The 1980 election marked a decisive change in political direction by the American people and a rejection of big government and the welfare state.

Reagan campaigned on the promise to restore American strength and pride and to reduce government's role in people's lives. He won by a landslide.

## The Evolution of the American Welfare State

During the 1930s, the United States experienced the Great Depression. It was a time of numerous business failures and massive unemployment. To help the nation recover, President Franklin Roosevelt created many new federal programs. These programs, collectively known as the New Deal, represented a great change in the role of government. Until then, Americans had depended on families and local communities to help with problems of hunger, poverty, and unemployment. With the New Deal, Washington took the lead in such aid.

This effort was repeated in the 1960s. President Lyndon Johnson created a new set of federal programs. They aimed to end poverty, improve health care, and solve many other social problems.

As the years went on and not all the problems were solved, many people began to question these programs. People also objected to paying the taxes necessary to operate "big government." They resented making welfare payments to people whom they considered freeloaders.

Conservatives in the Republican Party organized this growing opposition. Their candidate, Arizona senator Barry Goldwater, lost the 1964 presidential election, but the movement continued to grow. In 1980, the Republicans nominated another conservative candidate: Ronald Reagan.

## A Victory for Conservatives

Ronald Reagan campaigned on the promise to "get government off the backs of the people." He vowed to reduce the size and scope of the federal government and cut the federal budget. Reducing taxes, he said, would leave Americans more money to spend on goods and services, which, in turn, would create more jobs. Reagan also promised to reduce government regulation of business.

Reagan was elected in a landslide victory. He won 44 of 50 states. In his inaugural address he said, "Government is not the solution to our problems; government is the problem." Cheerful and optimistic, Reagan had the ability to make Americans feel good. Time and again, he appealed to traditional American values of hard work, individual responsibility, and

The Reagan years were a time of contrast. Many succeeded—especially in the stock market and in real estate—but many others were forced out of their homes.

patriotism as the means to prosperity and happiness. His concept of limited federal government—called the New Federalism—proved extremely popular, and in 1984 he was elected to a second term. This time he won 49 of 50 states!

During Reagan's two terms, taxes were lowered. The responsibility for government social programs was shifted from federal to state and local governments. Cuts were made in social welfare payments, such as federal Medicare payments, unemployment compensation, and food stamps. At the same time, the defense budget was increased as part of a peace-through-strength strategy.

The Reagan administration continued the deregulation of the airline, banking, and trucking industries. In addition, there was also a general loosening of environmental and work safety regulations.

## After the Reagan Presidency

When Ronald Reagan left office in January 1989, two-thirds of the American people approved his performance as President. This was the highest approval rating for a retiring President since World War II. He could point proudly to sharp cuts in income tax rates, sweeping tax reform, reduced unemployment, and economic growth without rising prices.

Reagan's critics, however, questioned the effects of the "Reagan revolution." Reagan's tax policies, they said, helped the rich get richer. The poor and middle class were not as well off as before. Also, under the New Federalism, state and local governments had difficulty funding social programs. Many programs had to be cut, leading to a rise in the number of homeless people. Federal deregulation resulted in many airline bankruptcies. And widespread greed and corruption resulted in the failures of thousands of savings and loan associations.

Ironically, the "Reagan revolution" did not reduce the size of government. When Ronald Reagan left office, the federal government employed more people than before. Government spending—and debt—had soared to gigantic size.

George Bush, elected to the presidency in 1988, continued Reagan's policies. But by 1992, most Americans wanted a change from Reaganomics—as the Republican economic policies came to be called. Democrat Bill Clinton, campaigning on a platform of change, won the 1992 election. Clinton's goals include making government more involved and more responsible for the general welfare of Americans—a partial reversal of the Reagan policies.

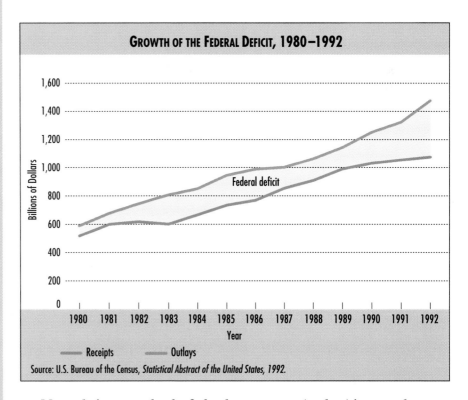

**GROWTH OF THE FEDERAL DEFICIT, 1980–1992**

Federal deficit

Receipts     Outlays

Source: U.S. Bureau of the Census, *Statistical Abstract of the United States, 1992.*

**Money being spent by the federal government (outlays) increased at a greater rate than money coming in (receipts), thereby increasing the deficit. To cover that deficit, the government had to borrow vast sums of money. President Clinton has vowed to reduce the deficit.**

43

# Glossary

**abolitionist:** A person who wanted to end slavery.

**amendment:** A change or correction; an addition to the U.S. Constitution.

**armistice:** An agreement to stop fighting temporarily.

**boycott:** The refusal to use a service or product in order to achieve a desired political or economic goal.

**checks and balances:** The system set up by the U.S. Constitution in which power is shared by three branches of government so that no one branch will have too much power.

**civil war:** A war between two groups within the same country.

**Cold War:** The hostility without actual fighting that existed between the United States and the Soviet Union from the end of World War II until the fall of communism in 1990.

**communism:** A socialist system practiced in the former Soviet Union and other countries, in which all factories, businesses, and farms are controlled by the state.

**compact:** An agreement between two or more parties.

**democracy:** A government in which the people rule, usually through elected representatives.

**depression:** A period of low economic production and high unemployment.

**deregulation:** The process of removing rules and restrictions.

**disarmament:** The giving up or reducing of armed forces and weapons.

**discrimination:** Unfair treatment because of prejudice such as racism.

**egalitarian:** Favoring equal rights for all.

**electoral college:** A group of persons elected by U.S. voters to formally elect the President and Vice-President.

**emancipation:** The act of freeing the African American slaves.

**federal:** Consisting of a group of states or other units under a central government.

**guerrilla:** A member of a small group of irregular soldiers who make surprise raids on an enemy army.

**imperialism:** A policy of maintaining an empire; trying to seize more territory or control over other countries to acquire raw materials or markets for trade.

**indentured servant:** A person from England or another country who promised to work for an employer for a certain length of time in return for free passage to one of the American colonies.

**inflation:** The economic condition of rising prices.

**injunction:** A court order to refrain from some action.

**integrate:** To end segregation; to open an organization or facility to all races.

**isolationist:** A person who believes that a country should not become involved in the affairs of other nations.

**militia:** An army of citizens who will be called out only in case of an emergency.

**monarchy:** A country ruled by a monarch such as a king or queen.

**nationalism:** A spirit of patriotism or support for a particular nation or cultural group.

**negotiate:** To come to terms or reach an agreement through discussion.

**neutral:** Refusing to take sides in a war.

**passive resistance:** Opposition to a government or police force by refusing to cooperate or by holding peaceful demonstrations.

**progressive:** Favoring reforms in political or social institutions, such as ending corruption in government or protecting the rights of workers.

**quota:** The maximum number of immigrants that may be admitted into a country.

**radical:** Tending toward extreme changes from what is usual or traditional.

**ratification:** Official approval.

**Reconstruction:** The reorganization of the former Confederate states that took place after the Civil War.

**republican:** Having a government without a monarch, usually one in which power is held by the citizens through their elected officials.

**secede:** To withdraw from.

**sedition:** Trying to create discontent with or rebellion against a government.

**segregation:** Separation, as of races, either by law or by custom.

**sit-in:** A type of demonstration used by civil rights workers and others, in which protesters sit (for instance, at a lunch counter) and refuse to move until their demands are met.

**Social Security:** The provision of income to the elderly, disabled, or unemployed.

**suffrage:** The right to vote.

**tariff:** A tax, usually on imports.

**temperance movement:** The movement to end the use of alcohol.

**welfare:** Government aid to disadvantaged groups such as the poor, the elderly, and the handicapped.

# Suggested Readings

★ ★ ★ ★ ★

**Note:** An asterisk (*) denotes a Young Adult title.

Allen, Frederick Lewis. *Only Yesterday: An Informal History of the 1920's.* Harper & Row, 1957.

————. *Since Yesterday—The 1930's in America: September 3, 1929 to September 3, 1939.* Harper & Row, 1940.

Bridenbaugh, Carl. *The Spirit of '76: The Growth of American Patriotism Before Independence.* Oxford, 1975.

Brown, Dee. *Hear That Lonesome Whistle Blow: Railroads in the West.* Holt & Co., 1977.

Cannon, Lou. *President Reagan: The Role of a Lifetime.* Simon & Schuster, 1991.

Commager, Henry Steele. *The Great Declaration.* Bobbs-Merrill Co., 1958.

*Faber, Doris. *The Birth of a Nation: The Early Years of the United States.* Scribners, 1989.

*Feinberg, Barbara. *American Political Scandals Past and Present.* Franklin Watts, Inc., 1992.

Fitzgerald, Francis. *Fire in the Lake: The Vietnamese and the Americans in Viet Nam.* Random House, 1973.

Garthoff, Raymond L. *Reflections on the Cuban Missile Crisis.* Brookings, 1989.

Goldston, Robert. *The Coming of the Civil War.* Macmillan, 1972.

Gurko, Miriam. *The Ladies of Seneca Falls: The Birth of the Woman's Rights Movement.* Schocken, 1987.

Hosmer, James K. *The History of the Louisiana Purchase.* Reprint Services, 1992.

*Lawson, Don. *The United States in the Spanish-American War.* Harper & Row, 1976.

*Lester, Julius. *To Be a Slave.* Dial Books, 1968.

*Levinson, Nancy S. *The First Women Who Spoke Out.* Dillon, 1983.

*Lindrop, Edmund. *Assassinations That Shook America.* Franklin Watts, Inc., 1992.

*Lomask, Milton. *The Spirit of 1787: The Making of Our Constitution.* Farrar, Straus & Giroux, 1980.

*Lord, Walter. *Day of Infamy.* Bantam, 1991.

*Mabie, Margot C. J. *Vietnam There and Here.* Henry Holt & Co., 1985.

*Peavy, Linda, and Smith, Ursula. *Women Who Changed Things.* Scribners, 1983.

*Railroaders, The.* Time-Life, 1973.

Williams, Juan. *Eyes on the Prize: America's Civil Rights Years, 1954–1965.* Viking Penguin, 1988.

# Index

★ ★ ★ ★ ★